Contents

MAMMALS

CHITAL

Chital become reproductively mature when they are 12 to 14 months old. Breeding is non-seasonal, occurring all year round. Following a gestational period of 210 to 225 days, the female gives birth to 1 to 2 young ones. The young are usually hidden for up to a week after being born. At birth, the young weigh around 3 kilograms and are nursed until they attain six months.

Appearance

They have a golden to rufous coat with white spots. Their abdomens, throats, rumps, tails, the inside of their legs and their tails are white. Running along their spine are black stripes. Present on each of their antlers are three lines that can be up to 1 meter long. They antlers are usually shed annually and are only present on males. Their tails measures about 20 centimeters long and usually have dark stripes stretching their entire length. Adults weigh 98 to 110 kilograms.

Lifespan

They have a lifespan of 20 to 30 years.

Length

Adult males have a shoulder height of 90 to 100 centimeters while females measure 65 to 75 centimeters. Head to body length of adult males and females is around 1.7 meters.

Diet

They are herbivores feeding on grasses, fruits and flowers.

HAWAAIAN MONK SEAL
Breeding

Female Hawaiian monk seals start breeding when they are around 5 to 10 years old. Breeding occurs from February to July. Following a gestational period of 10 to 11 months, the female gives birth to one young one. At birth, the pup weighs around 11 to 15 kilograms. Its coat is usually black during this time and it undergoes molting within 5 to 6 weeks. The young one is nursed for 5 to 6 weeks after which it is weaned before attaining independence.

Appearance

Hawaiian monk seals have grey coats and a slender physique. Their heads are small and relatively flat and their eyes are large and black. They possess a U-shaped wide muzzle that appears flattened. They also have smooth vibrissae

3

that may be long or short with a black base and yellowish-white tips. During their molting season, their coats fade to cream or light silver-grey above. The young usually have a black coat at birth. Adults weigh 140 to 270 kilograms.

Lifespan

They have a lifespan of 25 to 30 years.

Length

Adults measure between 2 to 2.4 meters long.

Diet

They are carnivores feeding on fish, squid, octopuses, crabs, lobsters and cephalopods.

SPINNER DOLPHIN

Breeding

Males attain reproductive maturity when they are 10 to 12 years old while females become reproductively mature when they are 5 to 10 years old. Breeding occurs all year round.

Following a gestational period of 10 months, the female gives

birth to one calf. The young nurse for up to 2 years but are weaned when they are 6 months old. They usually attain independence thereafter.

Appearance

Spinner dolphins are small in size with a long and slender beak and on their dorsum, there is a triangular fin. Most of these dolphins are dark grey on their backs and their under sides have a light grey appearance that may also be white. A dark grey band runs from their eye to the flipper and it usually has a fringe of a thin light stripe. Adults weigh about 75 kilograms.

Lifespan

They live for 20 to 25 years.

Length

Adults measure between 1 to 2.4 meters long.

Diet

They are carnivores feeding on fish, shrimp and squid.

MULE DEER
Breeding

Mule deer attain reproductive maturity when they are 18 months although mating starts when they are 3 to 4 years old. Breeding occurs from November to February and after a gestational period of 6 to 7 months, the female gives birth to 1 to 2 young ones. The mother nurses her young ones and hides them during the day and within a few weeks, the young are capable of following their mother. At around 5 weeks, the fawns are weaned and weaning is complete at around 16 weeks. They remain with their mother until they are one year old at which time they become independent.

Appearance

The coat of mule deer usually varies depending on the season.
In summer, it is usually tannish-brown and it becomes
brownish-grey in winter. Present on their rumps is a white patch
and their tails are small with a white appearance and a black
tip. Males also possess antlers which are usually forked.
The antlers are often shed but usually regrow immediately.
Females do not possess antlers. The young have a spotted coat.
Adults weigh 43 to 150 kilograms.

Lifespan

They live for around 9 to 20 years.

Length

Adults have a shoulder height of 80 to 106 centimeters and
measure between 1 to 2 centimeters long.

Diet

They are herbivores feeding on tree branches, grasses, twigs, grapes, ferns, mushrooms, raspberry vines and mistletoe.

PYGMY KILLER WHALE
Breeding

Very little data is available on their mating system although the female gives birth to one young one. She solely cares for the young one until it attains independence. The young often form groups. There is little information on when weaning occurs and when the young become independent.

Appearance

Pygmy killer whales have a stout body that is dark grey-black. Their underbelly appears significantly lighter. Their heads are blunt and lack a beak. They possess a dorsal fin that is located at the center of their bodies. Their flippers have rounded tips and are moderate in length. They also have a sub triangular dorsal fin that points slightly backwards. An extending groove is present running from their umbilicus to the anus. Adults weigh 110 to 170 kilograms.

Lifespan

Pygmy killer whales live for about 21 years.

Length

Adults measure between 2.1 to 2.6 meters long.

Diet

They are carnivores feeding on octopus, fish, squid, tuna, mollusks and dolphins.

SPERM WHALE
Breeding

Sperm whales attain reproductive maturity at around 10 years. Breeding occurs from January to August with a peak from March to June. Following a gestational period of 14 to 16 months, the female gives birth to one calf.

Appearance

Sperm whales have a large head that is block-shaped. Located close to the front of the head is an S-shaped blowhole which is usually shifted to the left. These whales also possess thick triangular tail lobes that are very flexible. A series of ridges are present on their backs caudal third and the largest ridge is known as a hump. The skin on their backs appears wrinkled. Adults weigh 12 to 40 tons.

Lifespan

Sperm whales live for around 70 years.

Length

Adult sperm whales measure between 11 to 18 meters long.

Diet

They are carnivores feeding on fish, sharks, octopi, squid and skates.

DENSE-BEAKED WHALE
Breeding

Dense-beaked whales attain reproductive maturity when they are around 9 years old. Following a gestational period of around 12 months, the female gives birth to one calf that is nursed for up to a year. The female primarily cares for the young one until it becomes independent.

Appearance

These whales have long and narrow bodies with long beaks and throat grooves on their lower jaws. They appear dark blue to grey on their upper parts and are light grey on their underside. Their heads are brown in color with a light grey coloration around their jaws and lips. Adults weigh 800 to 1000 kilograms.

Lifespan

They live for up to 27 years.

Length

Adults measure between 4.4 to 4.6 meters long.

Diet

They are carnivores feeding on fish, mollusks, squid and cephalopods.

FIN WHALE
Breeding

Fin whales attain reproductive maturity when they are around 4 to 8 years old. Breeding is seasonal, occurring from November to January. The female then gives birth to one young one following a gestational period of 11 to 12 months. The infant is nursed by its mother for 6 to 7 months after which it is weaned. It then attains independence when it is around 8 months old.

Appearance

These whales are the second largest mammals after the blue whales. They possess long bodies that are lean and brown-grey on their upper parts and deep white on their under sides. A medium-sized white patch is present on their lower right jaw and they have a distinct ridge on their backs which is due to the fact that the bases of their tails are raised. Their white underside usually wraps around their mid-section laterally. They possess two blowholes and a longitudinal ridge extends from the tip of their snouts to the beginning of their blowholes. Adults weigh up to 70000kilograms.

Lifespan

Fin whales live for around 75 years.

Length

Adults measure between 19 to 27 meters long.

Diet

Fin whales are carnivores feeding on fish, aquatic crustaceans, zooplankton and phytoplankton.

BRUSH-TAILED ROCK WALLABY
Breeding

Brush-tailed rock-wallabies become reproductively mature when they are around 18 months old. Breeding is non-seasonal, occurring throughout the year. The female then gives birth to tone young one following a gestational period of 31 days. The young one crawls to its mother's pouch after birth for up to 29 weeks. While in this pouch, the mother often provides care for and feeds the young one. Upon evacuating the pouch, it continues suckling for around 3 months and is

weaned when it attains 7 months. It attains independence thereafter.

Appearance

These animals appear dull-brown on their backs and have a pale coloration on their chests and bellies as well as their rumps. Their feet are usually furry and black. Extending as a dark stripe to the margin of their hind legs is a black axillary patch. Their tails appear darker distally and have a prominent brush. They also have long, thick pelage around their rumps, flanks and tail bases although animals in northern ranges have a lighter appearance and a less prominent tail brush. Their tails are also quite long as compared to their head and body length. Adults weigh around 4 to 10 kilograms.

Lifespan

They have a lifespan of up to 11 years.

Length

Adults measure between 45 to 58 centimeters long.

Diet

They are herbivores feeding on leaves, seeds, fruit, grains, nuts, bark, stems and wood.

PYGMY SPERM WHALE
Breeding

Pygmy sperm whales attain reproductive maturity when they are 4 to 5 years old. Breeding occurs from March to August. Following a gestational period of 9 to 11 months, the female gives birth to one young one. At birth the young weigh about 50 kilograms and are around 1.2 meters long. They nurse for around one year after which they are weaned before becoming independent.

Appearance

The body of pygmy sperm whale is small and compact with a small rounded dorsal fin. Their heads have a conical and pointed snout with a small, narrow and distinct lower jaw. They have dark bulging eyes with a light circular mark above and around the eyes. A pale false gill plate is present behind their eye. Situated slightly to the left side of their bodies is a single blowhole. Their upper pars appear black to bluish-grey and is light grey on the sides. Their underside is pale with whitish to pinkish coloration. Adults weigh around 700 to 1000 grams.

Lifespan

They live for up to 23 years.

Length

Adults measure up to 4.8 meters in body length.

Diet

They are carnivores feeding on squid, octopus, fish, shrimp and crabs.

INDO-PACIFIC BEAKED WHALE
Breeding

There is no information on the breeding season of Indo-pacific beaked whale. Following a gestational period of 18 to 24 months, the female gives birth to one young one. The young one is cared for by its mother until it attains independence.

Appearance

Indo-pacific beaked whales have large bodies with a large hooked dorsal fin which is usually located behind the midpoint of their back. Their flippers are dark, small, narrow and rounded and their foreheads are well defined. They may possess a crease which distinguishes the forehead from the beak. Their blow is small, low and bushy and they range from dark grey, to bronze to brown to olive in color with this coloration extending from their blowhole and eye down their back and to their facial band. They have a lighter coloration on their forehead and a defined patch is present between their necks and abdomens with a lighter coloration that may be creamy or pale. They have a dark appearance on the upper surface of their fluke with their underside having several light streaks. The upper jaw of their beak is darker as compared to their lower jaw. Adults weigh about 2200 kilograms.

Lifespan

They live for about 40 years.

Length

Adults measure between 4 to 9 meters in body length.

Diet

They are carnivores feeding on feeding mostly on octopus and squid.

DWARF SPERM WHALE
Breeding

Breeding occurs in summer or winter. The female then gives birth to one young one following a gestational period of 9 months. The female cares for the young one until it becomes independent. The age at which the young one becomes independent is unknown.

Appearance

Their skin color varies and can be dark, grey, bluish grey or black brown and may be completely black with a light grey venter. They may also have speckled pink or purple blotches. Their flippers appear broad and have rounded edges and their tail fluke is sharply pointed. Located midway along the back is a dorsal fin whose shape varies from being triangular to curved and pointed. They possess a square head with a snout that is conical and pointed. On either side of their heads between the eye and flipper is a lightly colored crescent-shaped mark which is present between the eye and flipper which is called a false gill. They have grooves around their throat region with several short creases that are longitudinal. Adults weigh 135 to 270 kilograms.

Lifespan

They live for about 22 years.

Length

Adults measure between 2.1 to 2.7 meters in body length.

Diet

They are carnivores feeding on mollusks, fish and aquatic crustaceans.

NORTH PACIFIC RIGHT WHALE
Breeding

North pacific right whales attain reproductive maturity when they are 8 to 11 years old. They are seasonal breeders breeding in winter. Following a gestational period of 12 to 13 months, the female gives birth to one calf. The mother usually cares for her young one who nurses for up to one year before it is weaned and becomes independent.

Appearance

These whales have broad and robust bodies and appear disproportionate in size with their heads appearing proportionately large and taking up about one third of their body length. Their heads chins and lips have hardened layers of skin that are known as callosities. Their bodies are robust and broad with large and wide pectoral flippers. They appear black in color with a mottled appearance and they may have ventral patches that are white in color. Adults weigh 50 to 80 tons.

Lifespan

They live for around 50 to 100 years.

Length

Adults measure between 15 to 18 meters in body length.

Diet

They are carnivores feeding on krill, copepods, larvae of crustaceans and larvae of barnacles.

EDEN'S WHALE
Breeding

Eden's whales become reproductively mature when they are around 10 to 13 years old. Mating is non-seasonal, occurring all year round. Following a gestational period of 10 to 12 months, the female gives birth to one young one. She cares for and nurses the young one for up to 6 months solely. At 6 months, the young one is weaned and attains independence thereafter.

Appearance

These whales have sleek bodies with slender and pointed flippers. Their heads comprise a quarter of their body length. Their dorsal fin is hooked and is located about two thirds back on the body. They have a broad fluke and several throat grooves on their underside. Males appear notably smaller than females.

Lifespan

They live for around 50 to 70 years in the wild.

Length

Adults measure between 12 to 14 meters in length.

Diet

They are carnivores feeding on mollusks, fish, zooplankton, aquatic crustaceans and other marine invertebrates.

STRIPED DOLPHIN
Breeding

Female striped dolphins attain reproductive maturity when they are 5 to 13 years old while males become reproductively mature when they are 7 to 15 years old. Breeding occurs in winter and early summer. The female gives birth to one calf following a gestational period of 12 to 13 months. At birth the young are around90 to 100 centimeters long and weigh about 11 kilograms. The calves are nursed for up to 16 months. Weaning commences at 16 months and they become independent thereafter.

Appearance

Striped dolphins possess spindle shaped bodies with a long beak. They have a blue appearance and running along their spine is light grey to white stripes. Their bellies range in color from blue to white or pink. Extending from a ring around the eye are two black stripes and one of these continues on to the flipper while the other one divides into a short lower section. They also possess sickle-shaped dorsal fins and long flippers that are slim. Adults weigh 150 to 160 kilograms.

Lifespan

They live for around 55 to 60 years.

Length

Adults measure between 2.4 to 2.6 meters long.

Diet

They are carnivores feeding on cephalopods, crustaceans and fish.

GREY WHALE
Breeding

Grey whales become reproductively mature when they are 6 to 12 years old. Breeding is non-seasonal, occurring all-year round. The female then gives birth to one young one after a gestational period of 13 to 14 months. The young one is cared for by the mother and nurses for up to 6 months. Weaning commences at around 6 to 7 months and the young one becomes independent thereafter. They often inherit their mother's feeding ground.

Appearance

The backs of grey whales are mottled grey with small eyes above the corners of their mouths. They possess broad paddle shaped pectoral flippers which have pointed tips. A dorsal hump is present on their backs with up to 12 small bumps being located between the tail flukes and the dorsal hump. At birth, calves usually have a dark grey appearance but become lighter with age. These whales are often covered with whale lice and barnacles that are mostly concentrated on their heads and tails. Adults weigh about 41 tons.

Lifespan

They live for around 25 to 80 years in the wild.

Length

Adult females measure between 11 to 15 meters long while males measure about 11 to 14 meters in length.

Diet

They are carnivores feeding on eggs, mollusks, fish, zooplankton, cniridians, aquatic crustaceans and other marine invertebrates.

WILD BOAR
Breeding

Wild boars attain reproductive maturity when they are around 18 months old. Breeding occurs in autumn. Following a gestational period of 112 to 115 days, the female gives birth to 3 to 12 young ones. Prior to giving birth, she constructs a nest where the piglets will be born. At birth, the young possess stripes for camouflage. The young ones remain in the nest for up to 10 days before joining the previous litters. They are nursed for 12 weeks after which they are weaned. They then remain with their mother and attain independence once the next litter is born.

Appearance

Wild boars are short and massively built with short legs that are thin. Their trunk is robust and short and a hump is present on the region behind their shoulders. Their neck is short and thick and their heads are large in size. They possess small eyes that are deep-set and their ears are broad and long. Protruding from the mouths of adult males are long canine teeth. In winter, these boars have long, coarse bristles which are under laid with short fur that is brown in color. Their coat color is dependent on location and age ranging from light brown in the young to rusty brown with pale bands that extend from the flanks and the backs in older individuals. Adults weigh 80 to 175 kilograms.

Lifespan

They live for around 2 to 27 years.

Length

Adults have a shoulder height of 55 to 100 centimeters and measure between 153 to 240 centimeters in body length.

Diet

They are omnivores feeding on nuts, fruits, roots, green plants, eggs of birds, small rodents, worms, carrion and insects.

COMMON BOTTLENOSE DOLPHIN
Breeding

Common bottlenose dolphins become reproductively mature when they are 5 to 15 years old. Breeding is non-seasonal, occurring throughout the year. Following a gestational period of around 12 months, the female gives birth to one young one. The young one receives care solely from its mother and is nursed for around 18 to 20 months. Females within a group usually help each other in caring for the young. The young one is weaned when it is around 20 months old but it remains with its mother until it is 5 years old at which time it becomes independent.

Appearance

The bodies of these dolphins are fusiform with front flippers, flukes and a dorsal fin. Their dorsal fin, which is set near the middle of the back, is tall and curved. Common bottlenose dolphins usually have a black to light grey coloration on their sides and their bellies are white and may have a pink hue. Adult males weigh around 500 kilograms while females weigh about 250 kilograms.

Lifespan

They live for round 25 years in the wild.

Length

Adult males measure between 244 to 366 centimeters long while females measure between 228 to 366 centimeters in length.

Diet

They are carnivores feeding on mollusks, fish and aquatic crustaceans.

HUMPBACK WHALE
Breeding

Humpback whales attain sexual maturity when they are 5 to 10 years old. Breeding is seasonal, occurring in winter. Following a gestational period of 11 months, the female gives birth to a single calf. The calf receives care solely from its mother and nurses for up to a year although weaning occurs at 6 months. They become independent at one year of age.

Appearance

Humpback whales possess bulky bodies with a thin rostrum and long flippers. Their dorsal fin is short and varies from being long and curved to being entirely absent. The upper aspect of their bodies appears black in color while their underside is white. The flippers vary in color from being entirely white to being white only on the under surface. Present on their heads and at the front edge of their flippers are bumps. Adults weigh up to 40 tons.

Lifespan

They live for 80 to 90 years.

Length

Adults measure about 15 meters long with females being around 1 meter longer than males.

Diet

They are carnivores feeding on copepods, plankton, capelin, herring, sand lances, mackerel and krill.

JAVAN MONGOOSE
Breeding

They attain reproductive maturity at around 122 (males) to 301 (female) days. Breeding occurs from February to September. Ale gives birth to up to 2 young ones following a gestational period of 49 days. The young ones are cared for by their parents and are weaned at around 5 weeks before becoming independent.

Appearance

Javan mongoose has soft fur that ranges in color from pale to dark brown and is flecked with golden spots. Their heads are long and have a pointed muzzle while their tail is robust and muscular at the base. They also have short ears and their eyes are brown to amber in color although they appear blue green in juveniles. Adults have mass of around 305 to 662 grams.

Lifespan

They have a lifespan of about 3 to 4 years in the wild.

Length

Adult females range from 509 to 578 millimeters while males range from 544 to 671 millimeters in length.

Diet

They are carnivores feeding on small snakes, rats, frogs, crabs, birds, insects and ducks primarily. They also feed on fruits.

REPTILES

GREEN SEA TURTLE
Breeding

Green sea turtles attain reproductive maturity when they are 20 to 50 years old. Breeding occurs between March and October. The female then lays 70 to 200 eggs in a large pit. The eggs hatch after 6 to 8 weeks and the young turtles use their flippers to come up to the surface. Upon hatching, the young usually head to the water. There is no parental care offered to the young and they are independent upon hatching.

Appearance

Green sea turtles are large in size and they possess a small head in relation to their body size. Their bodies are covered in brown scales that have a light-colored edge. Males possess long tails that stick out past their shell. The shells of these turtles are smooth and have plates that do not overlap. These have different shades of brown and their pattern changes with age. They appear lighter on their undersides. Adults weigh 68 to 190 kilograms.

Lifespan

They live for up to 90 years.

Length

Adults measure between 78 to 112 centimeters in body length.

Diet

They are omnivores feeding on jellyfish, mollusks, echinoderms, sponges, worms, algae, fish, fish eggs, sea grasses, leaves and tree barks.

BROWN ANOLE
Breeding

Brown anoles become reproductively mature when they are around one year old. Breeding is seasonal, occurring during summer. The female then lays 15 to18 eggs which she covers up to hatch. Within 6 to 8 weeks, the eggs hatch. The young are usually independent upon hatching, receiving no parental care.

Appearance

Brown anoles have medium-sized bodies with a short snout and a short wide head that is usually covered in scales. Males range in color from light grey to stark black and may have a uniform color or multiple colors. They may have irregular dark patches with a light-colored network of lines outlining the patches. Females usually have a dorsal stripe that is white and a visible dark triangular pattern. Females also have variations in coloration. Adults weigh 3 to 8 grams with males being notably larger than females.

Lifespan

They live for up to 5 years in the wild.

Length

Adults measure between 35 to 68 millimeters in body length.

Diet

They are carnivores feeding on spiders, isopods, beetles, grasshoppers, flies, butterflies, crickets, moths, earthworms and snails.

GREEN ANOLE
Breeding

Green anoles attain reproductive maturity when they are 5 to 9 months old. Breeding occurs seasonally, from April to August. The female then lays eggs that are oval in shape and these hatches after a period of 5 to 7 weeks. Upon hatching, the young weigh about 0.27 grams. They are usually independent upon hatching, receiving no parental care.

Appearance

The scales of green anoles range in color from green to grey to shades of brown. They may also have a combination of these colors. They usually have the ability to change the scale color depending on external environment. Female green anoles usually have a line running along their dorsal surface from their necks towards the back. Males possess pinkish dewlaps which are usually located underneath their necks. Females lack a dewlap. Adults weigh 2 to 6 grams with males being notably larger than females.

Lifespan

They live for around 2 to 8 years.

Length

Adults measure 10 to 20 centimeters in body length.

Diet

They are carnivores feeding on beetles, flies, spiders, mollusks and arthropods. They also feed on grains, seeds and nuts.

CHINESE SOFT SHELL TURTLE
Breeding

Chinese soft-shell turtles attain reproductive maturity when they are 4 to 6 years old. Breeding occurs from March to September. Females then lay spherical eggs which are buried in soft soil. They hatch after a period of 60 days.

Appearance

Chinese soft shelled turtles' range in size from small to medium. Their carapaces lack scales and are leathery with the central part having a large solid bone beneath. Their carapaces are usually olive with dark blotches while the plastron has an orange-red coloration. The dorsal aspect of their limbs and heads are olive with the forelimbs having a lighter appearance and the hind limbs having an orange-red ventral appearance. Their heads have dark flecks with dark lines radiating from the eyes. The fronts of their tails have dark blotches and a black band is present on the posterior aspect of each thigh. Adults weigh about 6 kilograms.

Lifespan

They live for up to 30 years in the wild.

Length

Adult females have a carapace length of around 33 centimeters while adult males have a carapace length of around 27 centimeters.

Diet

They are carnivores feeding on fish, mollusks, crustaceans and insects.

OLIVE RIDLEY SEA TURTLE
Breeding

Olive ridley sea turtles attain sexual maturity when they are around 15 years old. Breeding occurs from June to December after which the female lays around 100 to 110 eggs. She covers the eggs with sand and following an incubation period of 45 to 65 days, the eggs hatch. Upon hatching, the young are immediately independent and do not receive any parental care. They usually find their way to the water upon hatching.

Appearance

Olive ridley sea turtles have an olive coloration on the outer aspect of their shell. Their shell is usually heart shaped and round. They also have scutes on the bridge of their carapace which each side having up to 14 marginal scutes. They possess a medium-sized head that is broad. The upper parts of these turtles range from greyish-green to olive with the young having a dark grey coloration. Present around the carapace of the young is a thin white line which forms a border on the carapace and trails the edge of the flippers. The posterior scute of olive ridley sea turtle is serrated. Adults weigh 25 to 46 kilograms.

Lifespan

They live for about 50 years.

Length

Adults measure between 62 to 70 centimeters in length.

Diet

They are omnivores feeding on fish, shrimp, mollusks, lobster, tunicates, crabs, snails, sea weed and algae.

LOGGERHEAD SEA TURTLE
Breeding

Loggerhead sea turtles attain reproductive maturity when they are around 35 years old. Breeding is non-seasonal occurring all year round with a peak between May and July. The female then lays 110 to 130 eggs which are incubated for 46 to 80 days. Upon hatching, the young are immediately independent receiving no care from their parents.

Appearance

They are the largest hard-shelled sea turtles and they possess a heart-shaped carapace. Their carapace is reddish-brown with olive tones and usually has five pairs of pleural scutes. They possess a cream to yellow plastron and as they age, two longitudinal ridges that are usually present on their plastron disappear. The skin of loggerhead sea turtle is dull to reddish brown dorsally and on the ventral aspect and the edges, it has a pale-yellow appearance. Males have browner skin and their heads have a yellower appearance as compared to that of females. The carapace of males is wider. Adults weigh 77 to 545 kilograms.

Lifespan

They live for 30 to 62 years in the wild.

Length

Adults measure between 85 to 100 centimeters in body length.

Diet

They are omnivores feeding on fish, mollusks, sponges, jellyfish, shrimp, cephalopods, fish, sea urchins, fish eggs, algae and leaves.

COMMON BOX TURTLE
Breeding

Common box turtle attains reproductive maturity when it is around 10 to 20 years old. Breeding occurs from April to October. The female then lays one clutch of eggs which often comprises of 2 to 8 eggs. The eggs are incubated in nests dug below the soil for about 3 months. Cooler nests produce males while warm nests produce females. The

young are immediately independent upon hatching.

Adults weigh 0.5 to 0.9 kilograms.

Appearance

Common box turtle is medium-sized with a high dome upper shell and a large hinged lower shell. Their carapace is brown in color and may have a variable pattern which comprises of yellow and orange lines and spots, bars or blotches. They also have a dark brown plastron that is uniformly colored and may have dark blotches. Their head is small to moderate in size with a hooked upper jaw. The iris of females is yellowish-brown while that of males is red.

Lifespan

They live for up to 100 years.

Length

Adults measure between 11 to 15 centimeters in length.

Diet

They are omnivores feeding on insects, berries, roots, flowers, amphibians and eggs.

GREEN IGUANA
Breeding

Green iguanas attain reproductive maturity when they are 3 to 4 years old. Breeding occurs during the dry season. The female then lays up to 65 eggs which are incubated for 90 to 120 days. The young usually possess an egg tooth known as caruncle, which they use to open the egg. Upon hatching, there is no direct parental investment on the young. They are immediately independent upon hatching.

Appearance

These iguanas range in color from green, lavender, orange, red, black to reddish-brown. They may also have a bluish coloration with bold blue markings. Present on their backs is a row of spines which is also present on their tails. They also possess a dewlap. Adults weigh around 9 kilograms.

Lifespan

They live for up to 8 years.

Length

Adults measure up to 2 meters in length.

Diet

They are herbivores feeding on leaves, flowers and fruits. They also feed on eggs, insects and terrestrial worms.

YELLOW BELLIED SEA SNAKE
Breeding

Breeding is non-seasonal, occurring all-year round and following a gestational period of 6 months, the female gives birth to 2 to 6 young ones. At birth, the young are around 220 to 250 millimeters long and are independent upon hatching. They are usually capable of finding food on their own.

Appearance

Yellow-bellied sea snake has a yellow under belly and a brown back. Its head is narrow and it has an elongated snout while the body is compressed. On its ventral aspect, there may be several black spots or bars. They also possess a paddle-tail, a valved nostrils and a palatine seal which aid them in their aquatic environment.

Lifespan

They live for around 2 years.

Length

Adults measure between 720 to 880 millimeters in body length.

Diet

They are carnivores feeding primarily on fish.

TROPICAL HOUSE GECKO
Breeding

Tropical house geckos attain reproductive maturity when they are around 6 to 12 months old. Breeding is seasonal, occurring from August to December, although it can occur all-year round. The female lays up to 2 eggs which hatch after a period of 22 to 68 days. There is no direct parental care that is offered to the young upon hatching and the young are immediately independent.

Appearance

These geckos are covered in black or brown bands and usually have the ability to change color based on light and temperature. They range in color from dark brown to grey to almost white. Tropical house geckos possess dorsal scales and their toe surfaces have spike-like scales. Adults weigh 4 to 5 grams with females being larger than males.

Lifespan

These geckos live for 3 to 5 years in the wild.

Length

Adult males have a snout to vent length of 43 to 59 millimeters while adult females have a snout to vent length of 40 to 60 millimeters. The average adult body length is 125 to 127 millimeters.

Diet

They are carnivores feeding on beetles, grasshoppers, centipedes, moths, spiders, isopods and cockroaches.

MOURNING GECKO
Breeding

Females are capable of reproducing without males. They produce up to two clutches of eggs throughout the year which are deposited in communal nests. After a period of 65 to 103 days, the eggs hatch. The male offspring may be produced but it is usually infertile.

Appearance

These geckos range from light to dark tan and have spots on their backs. A brown stripe runs from the ear to the tip of their nose. They are usually capable of changing their color to appear lighter or darker at different times of the day. Adults weigh

Lifespan

They live for around 10 years.

Length

Adults measure between 8 to 10 centimeters in length.

Diet

They are omnivores feeding on insects, fruit and pollen.

AMPHIBIANS

CANE TOAD
Breeding

Cane toads attain reproductive maturity when they are 6 to 18 months old. Breeding is non-seasonal, occurring at any time of the year. The female then lays 8000 to 30 000 eggs which hatch within 2 to 3 days. Upon hatching, tadpoles are immediately independent receiving no direct care from their parents. They metamorphose within 4 to 8 weeks of hatching.

Appearance

Cane toads range in color from brown or grey-brown to olive or reddish-brown. Scattered across their bodies are cream-colored spots and these are present on their sides, backs and legs. They possess cream-yellow undersides which may have black flecks.

These toads have bony heads and the bony ridges over their eyes meet above the nose. Their parotid glands are very distinct and are positioned behind the ears. They also possess warts on their bodies. Adults weigh about 1.5 kilograms with females being notably larger than males.

Lifespan

In the wild, cane toads live for about 5 years.

Length

Adults measure between 9 to 15 centimeters in body length.

Diet

They are omnivores feeding on beetles, honey bees, ants, crickets, winged termites, snails, small toads, snakes, algae and aquatic plants.

WRINKLED FROG
Breeding

Wrinkled frogs attain reproductive maturity when they are 1 to 2 years old. They usually breed in spring to autumn. The female then deposits 10 to 200 egg clusters with each cluster consisting of 400 to 1300 eggs. These hatch after a period of 5 days. Tadpoles are independent upon hatching receiving no direct parental care. Metamorphosis occurs within a year following hatching.

Appearance

Wrinkled toads usually have a dark

brown to greyish-brown appearance
and their skin is usually ridged and
warty. Present on their bellies are small black spots. Between
their eyes, there is a V-shaped marking. Males usually have a
dark grey throat that may appear black. Wrinkled toads have a
golden iris and diamond shaped pupils. They also have a bright
red appearance on the front and back aspects of their thighs.

Lifespan

They live for 4 to 5 years.

Length

Adults measure about 5 to 6 centimeters in length.

Diet

They are carnivores feeding on ants, crustaceans and arachnids.

GREEN FROG
Breeding

Breeding occurs in late spring. The female lays 1000 to 5000
eggs in clusters which hang from plants in water. Eggs hatch
after a period of 3 to 5 days and tadpoles metamorphose within
3 to 22 months. Tadpoles are usually independent upon
hatching, receiving no direct parental care.

Appearance

Green frogs can be greenish-brown, yellowish-green, brownish, green or even blue in color. They appear brighter on the front aspect and may have small random black spots. Across their legs, they usually have dark bands with white to yellow skin below the bands. The throat of males is bright yellow and they also possess a large tympanum. A well-defined back ridge extends from the back of their eye and traverses the entire length of their bodies.

Lifespan

They live for up to 10 years.

Length

Adults range from 7 to 12 centimeters in body length.

Diet

They are carnivores feeding on snails, slugs, spiders, flies, crayfish, butterflies, caterpillars, small snakes, moths and frogs.

AMERICAN BULLFROG
Breeding

American bullfrogs attain reproductive maturity when they are 3 to 5 years old. Breeding occurs from May to July. Females lay up to 20, 000 eggs which hatch within 4 days of being laid. Upon hatching, tadpoles are immediately independent receiving no care from their parents. They metamorphose within 3 years.

Appearance

American bullfrogs range in color from brown to green and may have white spots or blotches that are usually of a darker color on their backs. They possess webbed feet and the tympanum is located on either side of their heads close to the eye. It is usually larger as compared to the eye in male frogs. In females, it may be smaller than the eyes or of the same size as the eyes. In the breeding season, females have white throats while males have yellow throats. Adults weigh around 500 grams.

Lifespan

They live for 7 to 9 years in the wild.

Length

Adults measure between 100 to 175 millimeters in body length.

Diet

They are carnivores feeding on worms, insects, snakes, frogs, tadpoles, fish eggs, salamanders and crustaceans.

CUBAN TREE FROG
Breeding

Cuban tree frog females attain reproductive maturity when they are 255 days old while males become reproductively mature when they are 120 days old. Breeding occurs from May to October. The female lays up to 3000 eggs which hatch within 24 to 32 hours. Upon hatching, the tadpole is immediately independent receiving no direct care from its parents. Tadpoles usually metamorphose within three weeks.

Appearance

Cuban tree frogs range in color from light brown to white although they may have a green to dark brown coloration. Their abdomens are usually coarse with a white appearance. They possess bulging eyes and expanded pads on the end of their toes. Notably, the female is larger than the male and can be up to two times bigger than the male. Adults weigh about 57 grams.

Lifespan

They live for 5 to 10 years in the wild.

Length

Adults measure between 2.5 to 12 centimeters in body length.

Diet

They are carnivores feeding on brown anoles, other frogs, eastern narrow mouthed toads, lizards, southern leopard frogs, beetles and cockroaches. They may also feed on algae.

GREENHOUSE FROG
Breeding

Greenhouse frogs attain reproductive maturity at one year of age. Breeding occurs in spring and summer. The female lays 3 to 26 eggs which are attached to moist vegetation. These take about 13 to 20 days to hatch. Upon hatching, tadpoles are immediately independent.

Appearance

Greenhouse frogs range in color from brown to reddish-brown to bronze. Some may have a mottled coloration with a V-shaped band on their backs and in between their eyes and this band is usually faint. Most greenhouse frogs bear two stripes which begin at the eyes and terminate at the rear aspect of their bodies. They possess a light grey to white belly and their eyes appear red. Adult females are notably larger than males.

Lifespan

The lifespan of these frogs is unknown.

Length

Adults measure 12 to 30 millimeters in body length.

Diet

These frogs are primarily carnivorous feeding on beetles, ants, mites, cockroaches and spiders.

GREEN AND BLACK POISON DART FROG
Breeding

Breeding occurs between mid-July and mid-September. The female then lays 4 to 10 eggs in a moist and sheltered environment. The  eggs hatch after a period of 6 weeks and tadpoles wiggle onto the male's back so as to be transported to a pool of water. Upon undergoing metamorphosis, tadpoles leave the water and become terrestrial.

Appearance

These frogs are usually small to medium in size with a black to dark brown coloration as the background and this is patterned in shades of green. Some may appear black, brown or bronze on the background with patterns of light green, light blue, bright blue or bluish-white among other color variations.

Lifespan

In the wild, these frogs live for 3 to 15 years. **Length**

Adults measure 3 to 5 centimeters in length.

Diet

They are carnivores feeding on caterpillars, fruit flies, maggots, worms, centipedes, ants, termites and spiders.

BIRDS

RED-CRESTED CARDINAL
Breeding

Breeding occurs from October to November. The male constructs a nest prior to breeding where the female lays 2 to 5 eggs. These are incubated for 12 to 13 days. The young stay in the nest for 2 to 3 weeks and during this time, they are cared for by their parents. Once they are 2 to 3 weeks old, they become independent.

Appearance
Red crested cardinal is a medium-sized bird that usually has a red head with a white breast, belly and under tail. They have a grey appearance on the back, tail and wings. These birds also possess a red bib and a short crest that is also red in color. Their wing coverts have a grey appearance. Immature birds usually have a brownish-orange head as well as their bib. Adults weigh 30 to 35 grams.

Lifespan

They live for around 15 years.

Length

Adults measure about 19 centimeters long.

Diet

They are omnivores feeding on insects, berries, seeds and fruits.

COMMON MYNA
Breeding

Common myna attains reproductive maturity when it is around one year old. Breeding occurs from March to September. Both males and females take part in nest construction prior to mating. The female then lays 4 to 5 eggs which are incubated for 13 to 18 days. Incubation is primarily done by the female at night, while the male incubates during the day. Upon hatching, the young are blind and helpless and they are dependent on their parents for care. Once they are around one month old, they become independent and form flocks.

Appearance

These birds have a dark brown appearance with a black head. Their under-tail coverts are white in color. They possess yellow legs, bills as well as eye skin. Immature birds are browner on their heads as compared to adults. Adults weigh 82 to 143 grams with males being notably larger than females.

Lifespan

In the wild, they live for about 4 years.

Length

Adults measure between 23 to 26 centimeters in body length and have a wingspan of 120 to 142 millimeters.

Diet

They are omnivores feeding on rain, fruit, spiders, earthworms, crabs, nectar, flowers, lizards, mice and small snakes.

ZEBRA DOVE
Breeding

The breeding season of zebra dove is from September to June. Both the male and the female take part in nest construction prior to mating. The female then lays one to two eggs which are white in color. These are incubated by both parents in turns for 13 to 18 days. Both parents take part in caring for the young. At 2 weeks of age, the young fledge and become independent thereafter.

Appearance

Zebra doves usually have small slender bodies that are brownish-grey on the upper parts and bear black and white barring. They have pink under parts and the sides of their bellies, necks and breasts have black bars. They also have blue-grey faces and around their eyes, they have bare blue skin. Their tail feathers usually have white tips.

Lifespan

In the wild, they live for about 10 years.

Length

Adults measure 20 to 23 centimeters in length and have a wingspan of 24 to 26 centimeters.

Diet

They are primarily herbivores feeding on weed seeds and small grass but they can also feed on insects.

PACIFIC GOLDEN PLOVER
Breeding

Pacific golden
plovers attain
sexual maturity
when they are
around one
year old.
Breeding
occurs in
summer. The

female then lays up to 4 eggs which are incubated for a period
of 26 to 28 days. Both parents usually take part in caring for the
young although females are usually the first to abandon the
young once they learn to fly. Fledging occurs when the young
are 26 to 28 days old after which the young become
independent.

Appearance

Pacific golden plover is a medium-sized bird that is usually
yellow overall in winter with the yellow coloration being
present also on their breast and faces. They may have mottling
that ranges from black to brown. Their feathers have a dark to
light brown coloration with yellow spots and edges. They
possess a light brown head with white, black and yellow
mottling. Their chests have a light brown mottling which can
also be brown or white. Pacific golden plovers have black necks
and faces and these possess white borders. They also have dark
rumps and their legs and breasts are black in color. Adults weigh
102 to 108 grams.

Lifespan

In the wild, they live for 4 to 10 years.

Length

Adults measure between 23 to 26 centimeters in body length and have a wingspan of about 44 centimeters.

Diet

They are carnivores feeding on fish, mollusks, small reptiles, small mammals, insects and terrestrial worms. They also feed on fruit, seeds, nuts, grains and flowers.

BLACK-CROWNED NIGHT HERON
Breeding

Black-crowned night herons attain reproductive maturity when they are 730 days old. Following breeding, the female lays up to 4 green eggs which are incubated by both parents, in turns, for a period of 24 to 26 days. Both parents take part in caring for the young until they attain two weeks of age. At this time, the young fledge. At around the 6th to the 7th week of life, the young become independent.

Appearance

Black-crowned night herons have a white or grey plumage with short yellow legs and red eyes. On top of their heads is a black crown and their backs have a black appearance too. Extending from the back of their heads are two to three long plumes that are white in color. The bodies of these herons are stocky and their bills are short. Juveniles have a dull grey-brown appearance on their wings, backs and heads with several pale spots. They are paler with brown streaks on their underside and have yellow-green legs and orange eyes. Adults weigh about 800 grams with males being larger than females.

Lifespan

They live for about 20 to 30 years.

Length

Adults measure between 56 to 65 centimeters in body length and have a height of 63 centimeters. They have a wingspan of 43 to 46 inches.

Diet

They are carnivores feeding on chicks, bats, lizards, turtles, tadpoles, frogs, snakes, spiders, mollusks, crustaceans and eggs of other birds.

HAWAIIAN GOOSE
Breeding

Hawaiian geese attain reproductive maturity when they are 2 to 3 years old. Breeding is seasonal, occurring from August to April. The female then solely builds a nest and lines it with vegetation prior to mating after which she lays 1 to 5 eggs which are incubated for 29 to 31 days. Females solely incubate the eggs while the male guards the female during this period. Upon hatching, chicks are fully developed and receive care from both parents. They fledge once they attain 3 months and remain with their parents until they are around one year old at which time they become independent.

Appearance

They range in color from sepia to dark brown with their face and crown having a black appearance. Their cheeks are cream in color while their neck is buff and has black streaks. Their wings vary from brown to grey with white tips and the bottom part of their tails is black as is their beaks, eyes and feet. Adults weigh 1.8 to 2.3 kilograms with males being notably larger than females.

Lifespan

They live for about 28 years in the wild.

Length

Adults measure between 53 to 66 centimeters long and have a wingspan of 36 to 38 inches and a height of 21 to 26 inches.

Diet

They are herbivores feeding on seeds, leaves, fruits, nuts, flowers and grains.

WESTERN CATTLE EGRET
Breeding

Cattle egrets attain reproductive maturity when they are around a year old. Breeding occurs from April to October. The female then lays 2 to 5 eggs which are oval in shape and pale bluish-white. The eggs are incubated for 21 to 26 days by both parents in turns. Upon hatching, both parents take part in caring for the young. Once the chicks are about 30 days old, they fledge and become independent thereafter.

Appearance

Adults have a white plumage and yellow irises, bills and lores. Their chests and back plumes have a buff coloration and their legs range in color from green to black. The color of their plumage changes during the breeding season at which time they usually have long buff plumes on their crowns, their lower necks and lower backs. During the courtship season, their irises are bright red as is their legs and bills. Outside the breeding season, their legs are yellow-green and their irises are dark yellow. Their bills are yellow and have an orange base. Immature birds usually have a grey-tinged plumage and their legs are black in color. Adults weigh 270 to 510 grams with males being slightly larger than females.

Lifespan

They live for about 20 years.

Length

Adults measure between 46 to 56 centimeters in body length and have a wingspan of 88 to 96 centimeters.

Diet

They are carnivores feeding on crickets, flies, spiders, frogs, moths, earthworms, grasshoppers, crayfish, eggs, snakes, fish, nesting birds and eggs of other birds.

SPOTTED DOVE
Breeding

Breeding is non-seasonal, occurring all-year round with a peak from September to December. The female lays 1 to 2 eggs that are glossy white and these are incubated for 14 to 16 days. Both parents take turns to incubate the eggs. Upon hatching,

the young are helpless and are covered in pale down that is sparse. Both parents take part in caring for

the young until they are about 2 weeks old at which time they fledge. They then become independent.

Appearance

Spotted doves have a long and slim body with a grey coloration on the head and belly and rosy buff coloration below. A half collar is present on their back and the sides of their necks which are usually made up of black feathers that bifurcate. The bifurcated feathers have white spots at the two tips. They have dark brown wing feathers with grey edges and a white appearance at the center of their abdomens and vents. When in flight, their white-tipped outer feathers are visible. Immature birds have a dull appearance. Adults weigh about 160 grams.

Lifespan

They live for around 8 years.

Length

They measure between 28 to 32 centimeters in body length and have a wingspan of 43 to 48 centimeters.

Diet

They are primarily herbivores feeding on seeds and grains but they also feed on insects.

WHITE RUMPED SHAMA
Breeding

Breeding occurs from March to June. The nest is usually built solely by the female prior to mating. The female then lays 2 to 3 eggs that are pale green and have light brown and dark lilac spots. These are incubated for 12 to 15 days solely by the female. Upon hatching, both parents take part in caring for the young until they fledge and become independent.

Appearance

Adult females have a greyish-brown appearance while males have a glossy black appearance with a chestnut belly and white feathers on their outer tail and the rump. Both males and females have pink feet and a black bill. Immature birds resemble females but have a spotted chest. Adults weigh 28 to 34 grams.

Lifespan

They live for around 7 years.

Length

Adults measure 23 to 28 centimeters in body length.

Diet

They are carnivores feeding on ants, spiders, grasshoppers, worms and caterpillars.

HOUSE SPARROW
Breeding

Breeding occurs from early May to late September. Both males and females take part in nest building although the male selects the nesting site prior to mating. The female then lays 3 to 6 eggs that are white to greenish-white in color and may have brown dots. The eggs are incubated by both parents for about 11 to 14 days. Upon hatching, both parents take part in caring for the young until they fledge and become independent.

Appearance

House sparrows have short stocky bodies with a brown back and black streaks throughout their backs. Their underside has a pale buff appearance. The cheeks of males appear white and they also possess a black bib. These features are absent in females. They also have short legs and a thick bill. Adults weigh about 25 to 28 grams.

Lifespan

They live for about 13 years in the wild.

Length

Adults measure about 16 centimeters in length and have a wingspan of 76 millimeters.

Diet

They are omnivores feeding on seeds, grains, fruit, nuts and insects.

JAVA SPARROW
Breeding

Breeding occurs from February to August with a peak in April to May. Following nest construction which occurs before breeding, the female lays up to 8 eggs which are incubated for about 14 days. Upon hatching, both parents take part in caring for the young until they fledge and become independent.

Appearance

Java sparrows have a grey plumage on their upper parts and breast while their belly is pink. Their heads are black with white cheeks and a red eye ring around their eyes. Their feet have a pink appearance and their bills are thick and red in color. Juveniles appear brown on the upper parts and their under parts are pale brown. Their

heads are usually pale. Adults weigh about 25 grams.

Lifespan

They live for 2 to 7 years.

Length

Adults measure 15 to 17
centimeters in body length.

Diet

They are herbivores feeding on seeds and grains.

WARBLING WHITE EYE

Breeding

Warbling white eye attains reproductive maturity at one year.
Breeding occurs from February to December. The
female then lays 2 to 5 eggs that are white, smooth and
elliptical following nest construction. The eggs are incubated by
both parents for 11 to 12 days. Upon hatching, the chicks are
helpless and dependent on their parents for care. Both parents
care for the young who fledge when they are 10 to 12 days old.
Once they have fledged, the chicks remain with their parents for
15 to 20 more days before becoming independent.

Appearance

Warbling white eye has an olive-green appearance on its back and a pale green appearance on the underside. Their legs, feet and bill can be black to brown in color. They also have a yellow throat and a green forehead. The wings of warbling white eye are dark brown with a green outline and a distinct white eye ring is present around their eyes. Adults weigh 9 to 13 grams.

Lifespan

They live for about 5 years.

Length

Adults measure 10 to 11 centimeters in length.

Diet

They are omnivores feeding on leaves of flowers, fruits, insects and nectar.

NORTHERN CARDINAL
Breeding

Northern cardinals start breeding when they are one year old. Breeding occurs from March to September. The female builds a nest prior to mating where she lays 1 to 5 eggs that are white to green in color. The female incubates the eggs for 11 to 13 days and during this period, the male feeds the female. Upon hatching, both parents take part in caring for the young. When the young are 7 to 13 days old, they fledge but remain with their parents until they are around 25 to 56 days old at which time they become independent.

Appearance

Northern cardinals are medium-sized birds with males having a bright red plumage with a large black mask on their faces. Females have a light brown appearance with a reddish crest, tail and wings. Females also have a small black mask and bib. Both males and females possess a thick, bright orange beak that is cone-shaped. Immature birds resemble females but have black bills and a less red coloration. Adults weigh 42 to 48 grams.

Lifespan

They live for up to 3 years.

Length

Adults measure 20 to 23 centimeters long and have a wingspan of 30 centimeters.

Diet

They are herbivores feeding on seeds, grains, fruits and nuts primarily. They can also feed on carrion and insects.

ROCK PIGEON
Breeding

Breeding is seasonal, occurring from April to July and from August to September. The male selects a nesting site and brings building materials for the female as the female constructs the nest. The female then lays 2 eggs that are white in color and these are incubated for 16 to 19 days. Both the male and the female take turns to incubate the eggs. Upon hatching, both parents care for the young and feed them and within 35 to 37 days of hatching, the young are capable of leaving the nest. They usually return to the nest to roost for some time before becoming independent.

Appearance

Rock dove males have a pale blue-grey appearance on their upper parts, wing-coverts and mantle while their lower backs are greyish-white in appearance. Two black wing bars are present on their greater coverts and secondaries. Their under parts are pale grey while their chin is dark and their dark grey throat has green-purple gloss. Their breast has a similar appearance to the throat but usually has a stronger gloss and is bordered by a sooty-grey appearance below. Their belly and under tail coverts have a blue grey appearance while underneath their tails they are black with pale bases to their outer retrices. Their heads are dark-grey with the neck having an iridescence of glossy green-purple. They also have black bills and golden orange eyes to red orange eyes that have a pale blue eye-ring. Their legs and feet range in color from red to purple red. Females have a dull grey plumage with less neck iridescence. Juveniles appear dull with dull eyes and feet too. Adult males weigh around 370 grams while adult females weigh around 340 grams.

Lifespan

They live for around 6 years in the wild.

Length

Adult males measure 31 to 36 centimeters in length while females measure 29 to 35 centimeters in length. They have a wingspan of 63 to 70 centimeters.

Diet

They are herbivores feeding on nuts, fruit, grains and seeds.

RED VENTED BULBUL
Breeding

Breeding occurs from June to September. The female then lays two to three eggs that are pale-pink with dark red spots. Following an incubation period of 14 days, the eggs hatch. Both parents take part in caring for the young until they fledge and become independent.

Appearance

Red-vented bulbuls are medium sized birds with dark brown plumage with a scaly pattern and their head is black in color. They also have a red vent and a white rump. Their tails are long and black with a white tip. The distinguishing feature of these birds is their short crest which gives their heads a square appearance. Immature birds have a dull appearance. Adults weigh 26 to 45 grams.

Lifespan

They live for around 11 years.

Length

Adults measure about 20 centimeters in length.

Diet

They are omnivores feeding on fruits, nectar, insects, flowers and house geckos.

COMMON WAXBILL
Breeding

Common waxbills attain reproductive maturity when they are 6 to 12 months old. Breeding occurs from January to September and the female then lays 4 to 6 eggs which are incubated for 11 to 12 days. Both parents take turns to incubate the eggs. Upon hatching, both parents care for the young who are usually helpless at this time. Once the young are 17 to 21 days old, they fledge and become independent thereafter.

Appearance

Common waxbill is a small sized bird with grey-brown plumage and a red conical bill. They have a white-grey appearance on the cheeks, belly and throat with the rest of their plumage having fine bars. They are dusty red on their underside. The tails of these birds are quite long and their wins are rounded. Females usually have an overall pale appearance with a less red appearance along their bellies. The young appear duller than adults and lack the red coloration on their bill. Adults weigh about 8 grams.

Lifespan

They live for about 4 years.

Length

Adults measure around 11 centimeters in body length and have a wingspan of 12 to 14 centimeters.

Diet

They are herbivores feeding on nuts, grains and seeds.

WANDERING TATTLER

Breeding

Breeding occurs from May to August. The female lays 4 eggs that are olive-green and have brown blotches. These are incubated for 23 to 25 days by both the male and the female. Upon hatching, the chicks are fully developed and capable of leaving the nest. They are cared for by both parents for one to two weeks after which they become independent.

Appearance

The plumage of wandering tattlers varies in the breeding and non-breeding season. During the breeding season, their plumage is dark grey on the upper parts, the crown, hind neck, tail and wings. Visible on their upper tail coverts are narrow white tips which are also visible on their outer greater coverts and inner primary coverts. Their under parts are white and are marked with V-shaped dark grey bars with a small white area on their vent and central belly. They also have white throats, chins and foreheads with these parts having grey streaking.
Their under-wing area is dark grey with narrow white tips.

Present on their heads is a narrow supercilium that's white in color. Their bill is usually dark grey with a yellow base and their eyes are dark brown. Surrounding their eyes are two white crescents. These birds also possess yellow legs and feet. Outside the breeding season, they lack dark barring on their under parts and their chins, lower bellies and throats have a white appearance while the breast and flanks are dark grey. Immature birds have a similar plumage to that of adults during the non-breeding season. Adults weigh around 120 grams.

Lifespan

Unknown.

Length

Adults measure 26 to 29 centimeters in length and have a wingspan of 54 to 55 centimeters.

Diet

They are carnivores feeding on crabs, mollusks, crustaceans, worms and crabs.

GREY FRANCOLIN
Breeding

Grey francolins become reproductively mature when they are around one year old. Breeding is seasonal, occurring from April to September. The female lays 6 to 8 eggs that are incubated for 18 to 23 days. Both parents take part in incubating the eggs and in caring for the young upon hatching. The young stay with their parents until they fledge and become independent thereafter.

Appearance

Grey francolins usually have a barred appearance with a pale face that has a thin black border to their pale throat. Present on the legs of males are two spurs and these are usually absent in females. Adults weigh 200 to 340 grams with males being slightly larger than females.

Lifespan

They live for about 8 years.

Length

Adults measure about 26 to 34 centimeters long.

Diet

They are carnivores feeding primarily on termites and beetles. They also feed on grains and seeds.

COMMON GALLINULE

Breeding

Common gallinules attain reproductive maturity when they are one year old. Breeding usually occurs during the warm season after which the female lays 2 to 12 eggs. These eggs are incubated for 17 to 22 days. Incubation is done by both parents although males are the primary incubators. Upon hatching, the chicks are fully developed and are cared for by both parents. Once the chicks attain 50 days of life, they fledge and become independent thereafter.

Appearance

They range in size from medium to large and have a dark grey to almost black coloration and dull throats and chin appearance. The edges of their wings and rump are white while their legs are bright yellow-green. Their bills are narrow and have a frontal bright red shield. Adults weigh 192 to 493 grams.

Lifespan

They live for up to 11 years in the wild.

Length

Adults measure between 30 to 38 centimeters in length and have a wingspan of 50 to 55 centimeters.

Diet

They are omnivores feeding on leaves, nuts, fruits, grains, eggs, fish, carrion and insects.

LAYSAN ALBATROSS
Breeding

Laysan albatrosses become reproductively mature when they are around 8 to 9 years old. Breeding occurs from November to July. The female then lays one egg with a buff-white appearance. The egg is incubated by both the male and the female for a period of around 65 days. Upon hatching, both parents take part in caring for the chick and once it is 160 days old, it fledges. It becomes independent thereafter.

Appearance

The upper wing, mantle, tail, upper rump and back are black-grey while their under parts are white. A black smudge is present around their eyes and the pattern of their under wing is different from one individual to another. These birds possess pink bills that are dark-tipped with the bill of juveniles being grey in color. Juveniles also have a dark upper rump. Adult males weigh 2.4 to 4.1 kilograms wile females weigh 1.9 to 3.6 kilograms.

Lifespan

They live for 12 to 51 years.

Length

Adults measure around 81 centimeters in body length and have a wingspan of 195 to 203 centimeters.

Diet

They are carnivores feeding primarily on squid. They also feed on crustaceans, fish and coelenterates.

RUDY TURNSTONE
Breeding

Rudy turnstones attain reproductive maturity when they are around 2 years old. Breeding occurs from May to June. The female then lays 2 to 5 eggs which are incubated for 21 to 24 days. Both parents take turns to incubate the eggs with females being the primary incubators. Males usually defend the female as she incubates the eggs. Upon hatching, both parents take part in caring for their young ones. Once the young are 19 to 21 days old, they fledge and become independent thereafter.

Appearance

Ruddy turnstones are small sized robust birds with a reddish-brown plumage on their backs and wings. Their heads have black and brown feathers that are mixed with red feathers. They have bright orange legs and a white belly. A dark black band stretches across their necks and chests. They have stout upturned bills that are black in color. Adults weigh 84 to 190 grams.

Lifespan

They live for around 6 to 7 years.

Length

Adults measure 21 to 2 centimeters in body length and have a wingspan of 50 to 57 centimeters.

Diet

They are carnivores feeding on fish, eggs, carrion, aquatic worms, terrestrial worms, aquatic crustaceans, flies and their larvae and echinoderms primarily. They also feed on fruit.

YELLOW FRONTED CANARY
Breeding

Yellow fronted canaries attain sexual maturity at around 6 months old. Breeding is non-seasonal, occurring throughout the year but it coincides with the rainy season. The female then lays 2 to 5 eggs that are incubated for 13 to 15 days. Incubation is solely done by the female. Both parents care for the young upon hatching and at around 18 days of age, the young fledge. They attain independence when they are 18 to 24 days old.

Appearance

Yellow-fronted canary males have a golden yellow appearance on the face, flanks, belly, rump and tail coverts. Brown to black malar stripes and eye stripes continue through their beaks and are surrounded by golden-yellow coloration. Sparse dark streaks are also present on their backs. And their tail feathers are light brown to dark-colored with light yellow to green edges. Their tail feathers are light brown to dark colored with light yellow to green edges. They have pale pinkish-brown bills and are brown to yellowish olive-green on their back, crown and neck. Adult females resemble males but have a ring of brown feathers crosses the bottom of their throat. They also appear dull brown and paler yellow. Immature birds usually have heavy streaks. Adults weigh 8 to 17 grams.

Lifespan

They live for 1 to 7 years.

Length

Adults measure 11 to 13 centimeters in length and have a wingspan of 21 centimeters.

Diet

They are omnivores feeding on insects, worms, nectar, fruit, flowers, seeds, grains, leaves and nuts.

MUSCOVY DUCK
Breeding

Male Muscovy ducks attain reproductive maturity when they are 27 to 29 weeks old while females attain reproductive maturity when they are 26 to 28 weeks old. Breeding occurs from August to May. The female then lays 24 to 30 eggs which are incubated for 33 to 35 days. Incubation is solely done by the female although males and females take part in caring for the young upon hatching. Once the young are 60 to 70 days old, they fledge and remain with their parents until they are 10 to 12 weeks old at which time they become independent.

Appearance

Muscovy ducks have a brownish-black plumage with their dorsal plumage being iridescent green and purple. They also possess white wing patches. These sucks also have red fleshy protuberances on their faces. Adult males are larger than females and the mass of adults ranges from 2.7 to 6.8 kilograms.

Lifespan

They live for around 7 to 8 years in the wild.

Length

Adults measure 66 to 84 centimeters in body length and have a wingspan of 137 to 152 centimeters.

Diet

They are omnivores feeding on termites, crustaceans, millipedes, small fish, crustaceans, reptiles, leaves, wood, barks, stems, grains, seeds, nuts, and mollusks.

MALLARD
Breeding

Breeding occurs in summer and spring. The female then lays 5 to 15 eggs that are cream to grey to greenish-buff in color. These are incubated for 26 to 30 days. Upon hatching, the young are alert and are covered in down. They are usually capable of leaving the nest within 16 hours.

Appearance

During the breeding season, males usually have bright green heads and necks with a white ring at the base of their necks. Their chests are usually dark brown and the sides of their wings are grey in color. They also have a black and white tail and a yellow bill. Females usually have a mottled tan and brown appearance. Outside the breeding season, males also adopt this coloration. Their heads are a light shade of tan with dark streaks near the eyes and the crown. Their bills have an orange tint with dark markings. Non-breeding males usually have a yellow bill. A distinctive blue patch is visible near the shoulder of mallards when in flight. Mallards weigh 0.7 to 1.6 kilograms.

Lifespan

About 5 to 10 years in the wild.

Length

Adults have a body length of 50 to 65 centimeters and a wingspan of around 81 to 88 centimeters.

Diet

They feed on insect larvae, earthworm, grains and seeds.

WEDGE-TAILED SHEARWATER
Breeding

Breeding starts in February. The female then lays one egg which is incubated by both sexes for around 50 days. The chick is cared for by both parents until it is around 103 to 115 days at around which time it fledges. It then becomes independent.

Appearance

There are two morphs of wedge-tailed shearwater with the dominant morph in Hawaii being the pale morph. The pale morph has a grey-brown appearance on its back, upper wing and head and whiter plumage below.

Dark morphs are grey-brown all over their bodies. These birds possess a wedge-shaped tail and a dark bill. Their legs are salmon pink. Adults weigh about 340 grams.

Lifespan

They live for up to 29 years.

Length

Adults range in length from 43 to 48 centimeters and have a wingspan of 97 to 104 centimeters.

Diet

They are carnivores feeding on squid, fish and crustaceans.

WHITE TERN
Breeding

White terns attain reproductive maturity when they are around 3 to 5 years old. Breeding occurs all year round with a peak from late spring to early summer. The female lays a single egg that is speckled. The egg is incubated by both parents for around 36 days. Upon hatching, the chick is cared for by both parents. It fledges once it is 48 days old and becomes independent at around this time.

Appearance

The plumage of white tern is all-white and they possess a blue beak and small eyes which are often surrounded by black rings. Their tails are slightly forked. Immature birds have a brownish-red back and a grey colored neck. Present behind their eyes is a black mark. Adults range in mass from 100 to 140 grams.

Lifespan

They live for 16 to 18 years.

Length

Adults range in length from 28 to 33 centimeters and have a wingspan of 70 to 87 centimeters.

Diet

They are carnivores feeding on small fish, crustaceans and squid.

ROSE-RINGED PARAKEET
Breeding

Rose-ringed parakeets attain reproductive maturity when they are around 3 years old. Breeding occurs from December to January. The female then lays 1 to 7 eggs that are incubated for a period of three weeks. Both parents care for the young upon hatching. When the chicks are around 7 weeks old, they fledge but remain with their parents until they are 2 years old at which time they become independent.

Appearance

They are medium-sized birds that have a green plumage with a red beak. They possess long pointed tail and males often have a dark purple coloration around their necks. Females lack this ring around their necks or may show a shadow-like dark grey to pale neck rings. Adults weigh about 137 grams.

Lifespan

They live for 20 to 30 years.

Length

Adults measure about 40 centimeters in length and have a wingspan of 15 to 17 centimeters.

Diet

They are omnivores feeding on grains, seeds, nut, fruits, nectar and insects.

INDIAN PEAFOWL
Breeding

Indian peafowl becomes reproductively mature when it is 2 to 3 years old. Breeding occurs from April to September. The female then lays 3 to 5 eggs that are oval and brown in color. These are incubated for 27 to 29 days solely by the female. Upon hatching, chicks are fully feathered and are dependent on their mother for care. Fledging occurs within one week of hatching but the chicks remain with their mother until they are 7 to 10 weeks old after which they become independent.

Appearance

The male has a blue fan-like crest of wire-like feathers that are spatula tipped. It has a long tail that is made up of colorful eye spots. Females have a greenish lower neck and their plumage is dull brown. They lack the long tail that is present in males. Upon hatching, chicks are pale buff and have a brown mark on their nape connecting to the eyes. Juvenile males resemble females but have chestnut-colored wings. Adults weigh 2.7 to 6 kilograms.

Lifespan

They live for 10 to 20 years in the wild.

Length

Adults range from 0.86 to 2.1 meters in length and have a wingspan of 1.4 to 1.6 meters.

Diet

They are omnivores feeding on leaves, seeds, grains, flowers, nuts, roots and tubers. They also feed on insects, reptiles and terrestrial worms.

CHUKAR
Breeding

Breeding occurs from April to July. The female then lays 7 to 21 eggs which are incubated for around 24 days. The female solely incubates the eggs. The eggs hatch from May to August. Upon hatching, the chicks are fully developed. They are cared for primarily by the female although the male may also take part. The young remain with their parents until they fledge after which they become independent.

Appearance

They are medium-sized birds with a grey-brown coloration above and a buff-colored belly. Present across their forehead, eyes and down the neck is a dark black line which contrasts their head and breast from their white throats. Their flanks have bars that are black and white-chestnut while their outer tail feathers are chestnut. Their eyelid margins, bills legs and feet vary from corral pink to deep red in color. Immature birds have a mottled brown and grey appearance with slight brown bars on their flanks. Adult males weigh 510 to 800 grams while females weigh 450 to 680 grams.

Lifespan

They live for around 3 to 5 years.

Length

Adults range from 32 to 35 centimeters in length and have a wingspan of 51 centimeters.

Diet

They are herbivores feeding on leaves, seeds, nuts, fruits and grains primarily. They also feed on insects.

TIWI (HAWAIIAN HONEYCREEPER)
Breeding

Breeding occurs from May to July and may go from January to August too. The female then lays up to 3 eggs which she solely incubates for around 16 days. Upon hatching, the chicks are cared for and fledge when they are 22 to 26 days old. They then become independent three weeks after fledging.

Appearance

These birds are small to medium-sized and have a compact build. They are scarlet colored with black wings and tails. Some of these birds have a greenish plumage with males having yellow or orange markings. They also possess a long and curved bill which is usually salmon-colored. Juveniles have a golden colored plumage that has numerous spots. Their bills are ivory colored. They weigh 11 to 17 grams.

Lifespan

They live for 5 to 12 years.

Length

Adults measure 10 to 20 centimeters long with a wingspan of about 5 inches.

Diet

They are herbivores feeding on seeds, nectar, and fruits primarily. They also feed on insects.

GREAT FRIGATEBIRD
Breeding

Great frigate birds start breeding when they are 5 to 7 years old. Breeding occurs from December to September. The female then lays a single white egg which is incubated by both parents for 53 to 61 days. Upon hatching, both parents take part in caring for the young one who is usually naked, blind and helpless upon hatching. Once the chick is around 150 days old, it fledges. It then remains with its parents until it is 300 to 578 days old after which it becomes independent.

Appearance

Male great frigate birds have a black plumage and a red gular sac that is usually inflated during the breeding season. Their black feathers have a green iridescence upon refracting sunlight. Females are black in color with a white throat and a red eye ring. Their breast area is also white. Immature birds are black overall and have a rust-tinged white face, throat and head. Adult males are smaller than females and weigh 1000 to 1450 grams while females weigh 1215 to 1590 grams.

Lifespan

They live for around 25 to 30 years.

Length

Adults measure 85 to 105 centimeters in body length and have a wingspan of 205 to 230 centimeters.

Diet

They are carnivores feeding on birds, fish, mollusks and reptiles.

BLACK-NECKED STILT
Breeding

Black-necked stilts attain reproductive maturity when they are around 2 to 3 years old. Breeding occurs from February to August. The female then lays 3 to 4 buff-colored eggs that are dark spotted. The eggs are incubated by both parents for 22 to 26 days. Upon hatching, chicks are fully developed with their eyes open. They are capable of leaving the nest within two hours of hatching. They remain with their parents and receive care from them until they are 28 to 32 days old at which time they fledge. They become independent afterwards.

Appearance

They are slender-bodies birds with long necks and black and white plumage. They have dark bills that are long, lender and needle pointed. Males have glossy black upper bodies while females have blackish-brown upper bodies. The lower body, for head, cheeks and the sides of the neck are white in color. They have dark colored wings and a white spot is present over each eye. A white area is present over the bill. Their irises are crimson. Adults weigh 140 to 169 grams.

Lifespan

They live for about 20 years.

Length

Adults range in length from 33 to 41 centimeters and have a wingspan of 63 to 69 centimeters.

Diet

They are carnivores feeding on shrimp, crayfish, beetles, brine flies, grasshoppers, dragonfly nymphs, tadpoles, small fish and reptiles.

YELLOW-BILLED CARDINAL
Breeding

Breeding starts from October to February. The female then lays 2 to 4 eggs that are white to cream with brown streaks. These are incubated solely by the female for 13 to 15 days. Upon hatching, the young receive care from their parents until they are around 10 to 15 days old at which time fledging occurs. The young become independent thereafter.

Appearance

Yellow billed cardinals have a bright red head and a black throat. Their backs, wings and tails are medium grey while their under parts are white. They possess conical yellow-orange bills and their legs are also yellow-orange. Immature birds have brown-colored top parts and a brown-orange head. Adults weigh 17 to 24 grams.

Lifespan

They live for about 2 to 3 years.

Length

Adults measure about 15 centimeters in length.

Diet

They are herbivores feeding on seeds, flowers and fruits primarily. They also feed on insects.

CHESTNUT BELLIED SAND GROUSE

Breeding

Chestnut bellied sand grouse attains reproductive maturity when it is

around one year old. Breeding occurs from March to May. The female then lays 3 to 6 pale cream to buff-colored eggs that have brown spots. Both the male and the female incubate the eggs which hatch after 22 to 23 days. Upon hatching, both parents take part in caring for the young until they fledge and become independent within about 3 weeks of hatching.

Appearance

Chestnut bellied sand grouse is a short and compact built medium-sized bird with grey plumage on their backs and wings. Their breast and belly have sand-colored feathers and present on the belly is a chest-nut colored patch. Their heads are small and they possess rounded wings. Their beaks are short with a curved tip and their legs are short and strong. Adult females weigh 140 to 240 grams while males weigh 170 to 290 grams.

Lifespan

Unknown.

Length

They range from 31 to 33 centimeters in body length and have a wingspan of 48 to 51 centimeters.

Diet

They are herbivores feeding primarily on seeds. They also feed on shoots, bulbs, flowers and fallen berries.

AMERICAN WIGEON
Breeding

American wigeons attain reproductive maturity when they are one year old. Breeding occurs in spring and the female then lays 3 to 12 eggs. The eggs are incubated for 23 to 25 days by the female. Upon hatching, the young are fully developed and receive care primarily from their mother until they are around

37 to 48 days old at which time they fledge before becoming independent.

Appearance

In the breeding season, males have a mask of green feathers surrounding their eyes and a cream-colored cap extending from the crown to the bill. They also possess a white belly. When in flight, a large white shoulder patch is present on each wing. Outside the breeding season, the male resembles the female. Females have a grey and brown plumage. Both males and females have a pale blue bill that has a black tip, grey legs and feet and a white belly. Adults weigh 512 to 1330 grams.

Lifespan

They live for around 1 to 21 years.

Length

They range in length from 42 to 59 centimeters and have a wingspan of 76 to 91 centimeters.

Diet

They are herbivores feeding on leaves, seeds, fruit, stems, barks, wood and nuts primarily. They also feed on mollusks and arthropods.

GREYLAG GOOSE
Breeding

Graylag geese attain reproductive maturity when they are 2 to 3 years old. Breeding occurs from March to

May. Prior to breeding, the male and the female construct a nest. The female then lays 4 to 8 eggs which are incubated for about 28 days. Upon hatching, both parents care for the young until the following year after which they become independent.

Appearance

These birds have bulky bodies that are round and plump. The plumage of greylag geese is greyish-brown while their heads are darker and their bellies are paler in appearance. The outer edges of their feathers have a paler appearance too. Bordering the upper flanks is a white coloration and when they are in flight, their dark flight feathers contrast their light-colored coverts. Their legs and feet have a pink coloration while their bill ranges from orange to pink. Adults weigh about 2 to 4 kilograms with females being smaller than males. Immature birds lack spots on their bellies.

Lifespan

They live for about 8 to 10 years in the wild.

Length

Adults measure 74 to 91 centimeters long and have a wingspan of 147 to 180 centimeters.

Diet

They are herbivores feeding on leaves, roots, sprouts, grasses and fruits.

HAWAIIAN PETREL
Breeding

Hawaiian petrels become reproductively mature when they are around 6 years old. Breeding occurs from March to April. The female then lays one egg that is white in color. The egg is incubated for around 55 days. Upon hatching, both parents care for the young who remain in the burrow until they are about 4 months old. Fledging occurs once they are 110 days old after which they become independent.

Appearance

Their upper body is dark grey in color while their forehead and under parts are white. The wings have white appearance below and conspicuous dark margins. These birds possess flesh-colored legs and feet with black-tipped webs. Their tail is usually short and wedge-shaped. They also possess a greyish-black bill that is short with a sharp tip that curves downwards. Adults weigh about 430 grams.

Lifespan

They live for about 30 years.

Length

Adults measure about 16 inches long and have a wingspan of around 36 inches.

Diet

They are carnivores feeding on goat fish, squid, crustaceans, plankton, lantern fish and plankton

PIED BILLED GREBE
Breeding

Pied-billed grebes attain reproductive maturity when they are around 1 to 2 years old. Breeding occurs from April to October. The female then lays 2 to 10 white to turquoise eggs which are incubated for 23 to 27 days. Both the male and the female carry out incubation. Upon hatching, chicks are fully developed and are capable of leaving the nest within an hour of hatching. Both parents care for their young ones who are usually capable of swimming and diving immediately upon hatching. They remain with their parents until they are about 25 to 62 days old around which time they become independent.

Appearance

These birds usually have a dark brown plumage on their upper parts with a greyish coloration on the sides of their bodies and their necks. Present on their throats is a black patch and they also have a white-ring surrounding their eyes. They have thick bills that are bluish-white with one thick black stripe around the bill. Their under tail is white and puffy. In winter, they lose the black patch on their throats and the black stripe on their bill and their flanks and necks become reddish. Immature birds have light and dark stripes on their heads and necks but their plumage resembles the winter plumage of adults. Adults weigh around 253 to 568 grams.

Lifespan

In the wild, they live for about 5 years.

Length

Adults measure between 30 to 38 centimeters in length and have a wingspan of around 16 centimeters.

Diet

They are carnivores feeding on fish, insects, insect larvae, crayfish, beetles, minnows, sunfish, leeches and sticklebacks.

BARN OWN
Breeding

Barn owls become reproductively mature when they are around one year old. Breeding occurs all year round with a peak from March to June. The female then lays 2 to 11 eggs that are incubated for 29 to 34 days. During the incubation period, the female solely incubates while the male brings her food. Upon hatching, the young receive parental care from both parents until they attain 50 to 64 days old. Both parents continue feeding the young until around 5 weeks after fledging after which they become independent.

Appearance

They are medium-sized birds with light brown plumage that as variable black and white spots on their backs and heads. They possess large rounded heads that lack ear tufts. Their tails are short and their wings are rounded. The tail is covered with feathers that are white to light brown in color. Adult females are larger than males and weigh around 570 grams while males weigh around 470 grams.

Lifespan

They live for about 4 years in the wild.

Length

Adult females range from 34 to 40 centimeters in body length while adult males range from 32 to 38 centimeters in body length. Both adult males and females have a wingspan of 107 to 110 centimeters.

Diet

They are carnivores feeding on hares, rats, mice, voles, muskrats, shrew, birds and rabbits.

WESTERN MEADOWLARK
Breeding

Breeding occurs from mid-October to early April. The female then lays 3 to 7 white eggs that have brown spots. The female solely incubates the eggs for about 14 days. Upon hatching, the young are blind, naked and helpless with their eyes opening on the fourth day of life. Both parents provide care for the young. When the chicks are 10 to 12 days old, they fledge but remain with their parents for two more weeks after fledging before becoming independent.

Appearance

These birds have brown plumage on their upper parts that may have black streaks. Their under parts are yellow in color with a V-shaped black part on the breast. Their flanks are white with black streaks. The bills of these birds are pointed and long and their heads have stripes of light brown and black. Adults weigh 88 to 116 grams.

Lifespan

They live for 5 to 8 years.

Length

Adults measure between 16 to 26 centimeters in length and have a wingspan of 41 centimeters.

Diet

They are omnivores feeding on insects, seeds and berries.

BLACK FRANCOLIN
Breeding

Breeding occurs from April to June. The female then lays 10 to 14 eggs which she solely incubates for 18 to 19 days. The eggs range in color from olive to pale brown and they have white spots. Both parents take part in caring for the young who remain with their parents until after their first winter at which time they become independent.

Appearance

Male black francolins usually have a black plumage with a white patch on their cheek, white spots on their flanks and a chestnut collar. They have shades of golden brown with sub terminal tawny buff bands and pale edges on their backs and wings. Their tails are black and rounded with bars that are narrow white or grey. They have red-brown to red legs and necks. Adults weigh about 453 grams.

Lifespan

They live for about 7 years.

Length

Adults measure between 33 to 36 centimeters in length and have a wingspan of 50 to 55 centimeters.

Diet

They are omnivores feeding on termites, ants, berries, shoots, tubers, grains and grass seeds.

RED AVADAVAT
Breeding

Breeding occurs from January to April. The female then lays 4 to 6 eggs which hatch after 11 days. Incubation is usually carried out by both parents. Upon hatching, both parents care for the young until that are around 20 days old at which time they fledge. The chicks become independent thereafter.

Appearance

In the breeding season, males usually have a crown that is deep-red as is their backs and underneath their eyes, they have white streaks. They have a scarlet appearance on the sides of their heads, the breast and the underside. They appear dark red with white spots on the wings, flanks and tail over feathers and their tail feathers have a black coloration. Males have red beaks. In the breeding season, females are usually bright – yellow orange on the underbelly as well as the chest. Outside the breeding season, males resemble females and have a cream tan to cream yellow under belly and black streaks are present underneath their eyes. The crown, wings, backs and tails of females are dark brown and they also have fewer white spots as compared to males in the breeding season. Immature birds have a dull greyish brown overall appearance. Adults weigh 7 to 9 grams.

Lifespan

They live for around 7 to 10 years.

Length

Adults measure about 10 centimeters in length and have a wingspan of 49 centimeters.

Diet

They are herbivores feeding on seeds, grains and nuts primarily. They also feed on insects.

PALILA
Breeding

Palila attains reproductive maturity when they are around 3 years old. Breeding occurs from March to September. Both parents construct a nest after which the female then lays 1 to 4 eggs that are incubated for 15 to 17 days. The female solely incubates the eggs and is fed by the male during this period. Upon hatching, both parents take part in caring for the young until they are around 21 to 27 days old at which time fledging occurs after which the young become independent.

Appearance

These birds are large in size and have a white underside and a grey back. Their heads and breasts are yellow in color. They also have grey tail and flight feathers and these have green edges. Males usually have a brighter coloration on the breast and head with a distinct nape line existing between their back and head. Females appear dull greenish yellow on the head and neck and their nape line is indistinct. Males possess black lores that are dull grey in females. Adults have black bills and brown legs and irises. Immature birds are dull yellow on the head and breast with double barring on their primary and secondary coverts. Adults weigh about 35 grams.

Lifespan

They live for around 13 years.

Length

Adults measure about 19 millimeters in length.

Diet

They are herbivores feeding on leaves, grains, seeds, nuts, flowers, nectar and fruit primarily. They also feed on insects.

RED MASKED PARAKEET
Breeding

Breeding commences in March and eggs are laid at around June. The female lays 3 to 4 eggs that are white in color and incubates them for 23 to 24 days. Upon hatching, chicks are naked and blind and they are usually fully dependent on their parents for care. At around 6 weeks of age, they fledge but still remain with their parents for few more weeks before becoming independent.

Appearance

Red-masked parakeets have an overall green plumage that appears yellowish on the under parts. Their carpal edge, thighs, bends of wings and under-wing coverts has a red coloration. Their under-tail and under-wing appear yellow-green. These birds have red cheeks, heads, fore crowns and chins. Their bills are horn colored and hooked while their eyes range from dull yellow to brown or orange with a grey inner ring. They also have a cream-white eye ring around their eyes. The feet and legs have a grey appearance. Immature birds possess a green head that lacks red markings and their plumage is green with a few orange-red feathers on their carpal edge. They also have grey eyes. Adults weigh 165 to 200 grams.

Lifespan

They live for up to 25 years.

Length

Adults measure 29 to 31 centimeters long and have a wingspan of 53 to 55 centimeters.

Diet

They are herbivores feeding on fruit, seeds and flowers.

LAUGHING GULL
Breeding

Laughing gulls attain reproductive maturity when they are 2 years old. Breeding occurs from April to July. The female then lays 3 to 4 eggs that are green in color which she incubates for around 21 days. Upon hatching, chicks are usually fully developed and capable of leaving the nest within a few days of hatching. The young receive care from both parents and fledge when they are around 35 days old after which they become independent.

Appearance

They are medium in size with white plumage that is dark grey on the back and the wings. Their heads have a black coloration. They also possess long and red beaks. During the winter season, the black hood is lost. Juveniles have a mottled brown and tan appearance. Adults weigh 203 to 371 grams.

Lifespan

They live for 15 to 22 years.

Length

Adults measure 36 to 41 centimeters in length and have a wingspan of 98 to 110 centimeters.

Diet

They are carnivores feeding on shellfish, crabs, fish, insects, mollusks and young birds primarily. They also feed on carrion and berries.

SOOTY TERN

Breeding

Sooty terns attain reproductive maturity when they are around 6 years old. Breeding occurs all year round. The female then lays a single egg which is incubated for 28 to 30 days. Both parents take turns to incubate the egg. Upon hatching, both parents take part in caring for the young until they are around 2-month-old at which time they become independent.

Appearance

Sooty terns have dark black plumage and a white appearance on the under parts. Their bills are thin and black in color and they also possess a deeply forked tail and long wings. They also have black feet. Immature birds are blackish-brown on their head and chests with their upper parts having a speckled white appearance. Adults weigh 150 to 240 grams.

Lifespan

They live for 32 years.

Length

Adults measure between 33 to 36 centimeters in length and have a wingspan of 82 to 94 centimeters.

Diet

They are carnivores feeding on squid, fish, offal, insects and crustaceans.

BRISTLE-THIGHED CURLEW
Breeding

Bristle-thighed curlew starts breeding from mid-May to late May. The female then lays around 4 eggs that are olive buff in color and have brown markings. These are incubated by both adults for around 25 days. Upon hatching, the chicks are capable of leaving the nest. Both parents care for the young after hatching although the female leaves at some point and the male stays behind to guard the young until they fledge at around 21 to 27 days after which the young become independent.

Appearance

The upper parts of bristle-thighed curlew are dark brown with cinnamon-buff speckles while their rumps as well as the upper tail coverts are cinnamon in color. They are white in color on their bellies and lower breast and their upper breast and throats have a pale buff appearance with brown speckles. Their under wing has an orange-buff appearance with brown bars. These birds have broadly striped heads and bristle feathered thighs. A pale stripe runs down the center of their crown. Their bill is long and heavy with a downward curvature. Its tip is dark in color while the base is flesh-colored. These birds also have dark brown eyes and bluish grey legs and feet. Juveniles have conspicuous large cinnamon-buff spotting on their upper parts but otherwise resemble adults. Adult males weigh 254 to 553 grams while adult females weigh 372 to 796 grams.

Lifespan

They live for around 23 years.

Length

Adults measure 40 to 44 centimeters in body length and have a wingspan of 82 to 90 centimeters.

Diet

They are carnivores feeding on insects, spiders, mollusks, carrion and bird's eggs.

SHORT-EARED OWL
Breeding

Short eared owls attain reproductive maturity when they are a year old. Breeding occurs from late March to June with a peak in April. The female then lays 1 to 11 white eggs that are incubated for 21 to 37 days. Upon hatching, the young are helpless and are wholly dependent on their parents for care. Once they are around 24 to 3 days old, they fledge and attain independence within one to two weeks of fledging.

Appearance

Short-eared owls have yellow-white and dark-brown plumage and parts of their heads, legs and flanks are white. These owls have differently positioned right and left ears. Adults weigh 206 to 475 grams with females being slightly larger than males although it is not easy to tell males and females apart.

Lifespan

They live for around 21 years.

Length

Adults measure around 340 to 423 millimeters in length and have a wingspan of 950 to 1100 millimeters.

Diet

They are carnivores feeding on mammals and birds.

BLACK NODDY
Breeding

Black noddies attain reproductive maturity when they are 2 to 3 years old. Breeding is non-seasonal, occurring throughout the year. The female then lays one egg that is large with buff spots and reddish-brown streaks. The egg is incubated for 34 days and both parents take part in incubating the eggs. Once the chicks hatch, both parents take part in caring for them. They fledge when they are around 39 to 52 days old and remain with their parents until they are 116 to 171 days old at which time they become independent.

Appearance

Black noddies are medium-sized birds with a dark and sooty appearance and a white cap. On the lower and upper rims of their eyelids, they have small, white markings. They possess reddish-brown to orange legs and feet and a black bill. They also have orange-yellow mouth lining and tongue. Adults weigh 85 to 140 grams.

Lifespan

They live for up to 25 years.

Length

Adults measure about 35 to 40 centimeters in length and have a wingspan of 65 to 72 centimeters.

Diet

They are carnivores feeding on aquatic crustaceans, fish and mollusks.

HAWAIIAN HAWK

Breeding

Breeding commences from March to September. The female them lays one egg that she primarily incubates for 38 days. During this period, the male primarily hunts for food. Upon hatching, the female cares for the young and the male only visits when he is bringing food the young. When the chicks are 7 to 8 weeks old, they fledge but remain with their parents until they are around 30 weeks old at which time they become independent.

Appearance

Hawaiian hawks are of two-color phases, a light color phase and a dark color phase. In the light color phase, their head is dark while their under wings and breast are light colored. In the dark phase, their head is dark brown as is their under wings and breast. Their feet and legs have a yellowish appearance. In the breeding season, females usually have a yellow fore cap area. Juveniles have greenish feet and legs. Adults weigh between 441 to 605 grams.

Lifespan

They live for around 17 years.

Length

Adults measure between 40 to 46 centimeters in body length.

Diet

They are carnivores feeding on lizards, rats, birds and insects.

SANDERLING
Breeding

Sanderlings become reproductively mature when they are around 2 years old. Breeding occurs from May to August. The female then lays 4 eggs which both parents take turns to incubate for around 23 to 32 days. Upon hatching, both parents are involved in caring for the young who fledge when they are

12 to 14 days old. The young then become independent when they are 17 to 21 days old.

Appearance

They are small sized birds that have a pale plumage outside the breeding season. At this time, their heads are pale white and their upper parts are pale grey while their under parts are white. Present on their throat and breast is a dark shoulder patch. A white wing stripe bordered by black is seen when they are in flight. During the breeding season, they become reddish-brown on their upper parts and their heads adopt a deeper color. Immature birds resemble adults although their plumage appears darker on the upper parts. These birds also have black bills and adults weigh around 40 to 100 grams.

Lifespan

They live for about 13 years.

Length

Adults measure between 18 to 20 centimeters in body length and have a wingspan of 36 centimeters.

Diet

They are carnivores feeding on insects, eggs, mollusks, marine worms and aquatic crustaceans primarily. They also feed on leaves, roots, seeds, grains and algae.

ROSY FACED LOVEBIRD
Breeding

Rosy faced lovebirds attain reproductive maturity when they are 2 months old. Breeding occurs between February and May. The female then lays 4 to 6 eggs that are incubated for around 23 days. Females solely incubate the eggs while males feed them during the incubation period. Upon hatching, both parents take part in caring for the young. Once the young attain 42 days of age, they fledge and become independent when they are about 2 months old.

Appearance

Male rosy faced lovebirds have rosy pink foreheads, throats, cheeks, upper breast and chins with the rest of their bodies being bright green. Their underside appears lighter and their feet have a greenish-grey appearance. The bill of these birds has a horn-colored appearance. They also have bright blue feathers covering their tail and their rump is also bright blue. Tail feather is green in color and have blue tips. The rest of their feathers except those at the center have black bands with red patches near the ends. Juveniles have paler faces. Adults weigh 48 to 61 grams with females being larger than males.

Lifespan

They live for around 15 to 25 years.

Length

Adults measure around 15 centimeters in length and have a wingspan of around 99 millimeters.

Diet

They are herbivores feeding on grains, nuts, flowers and seeds.

APAPANE
Breeding

Apapane attain reproductive maturity at around one year. Breeding occurs from January to March. The female then lays 1 to 4 eggs that are white in color and have brown speckles. The female solely incubates the eggs while the male feeds her during this period. Upon hatching, the young are helpless and wholly dependent on their parents for care. Both parents take part in caring for their young ones. Once the chicks are 16 days old, they fledge but will remain with their parents until they are about 4 months old at which time they become independent.

Appearance

These birds have crimson feathers, black wings and a black tail. Their primaries may have white edges while their secondaries have crimson edges. They have brownish black thighs. The beaks of these birds are blue-black and they also possess a long tubular tongue. Immature birds have grey to brown buff appearance. Adults weigh between 14 to 17 grams with males being larger than females.

Lifespan

They live for about 11 years.

Length

Adults are around 13 centimeters in length.

Diet

They are herbivores feeding primarily on nectar but they also feed on butterflies, moths, lacewings, hoppers, bees, wasps, bark, lice, ants, beetles, true bugs, thrips and mites.

COMMON RAVEN
Breeding

Common ravens attain reproductive maturity when they are around 3 years old. Breeding occurs from February to May. The female lays 3 to 7 eggs that are incubated for 20 to 25 days. Incubation is solely done by the female. Upon hatching, both parents take part in caring for the young. At around 5 to 7 weeks of age, the young fledge and become independent at around this time.

Appearance

They are large in size with a black plumage and a ruff of feathers is present on their throats. The bases of their neck feathers are pale brownish-grey in color. Their tails are wedge-shaped and their bill is large in size and their irises are dark brown in color.

Juveniles usually have blue-grey irises. Adults weigh 689 to 1625 grams and females may be smaller as compared to males.

Lifespan

They live for 13 to 44 years.

Length

Adults measure about 54 to 67 centimeters in length and have a wingspan of 115 to 150 centimeters.

Diet

They are carnivores feeding on carrion, birds, reptiles, amphibians, insects, eggs and mammals primarily. They also feed on fruit, grains, nuts and seeds.

EASTERN ROSELLA
Breeding

Breeding occurs in spring to summer. The female lays 2 to 9 eggs which she incubates for around 19 days. The male feeds the female during this period. Upon hatching, chicks are helpless and wholly dependent on their parents for care. They stay in the nest for up to 32 days and continue to be fed with their parents for a short period after fledging before becoming independent.

Appearance

Eastern rosella birds have black feathers on their backs and shoulders with yellowish to greenish margins. Their wing feathers and those of the lateral aspect of their tails are blue and the tail is dark green in color. They have a red colored upper breast while the lower breast is yellow and fade to a pale green coloration over the abdomen. These birds also have grey legs. Females appear duller than males and have an under wings stripe that is notably absent in males. Immature birds appear duller than females and have an under-wing stripe. Adults weigh 95 to 120 grams.

Lifespan

They live for around 27 years.

Length

Adults measure about 30 centimeters in length.

Diet

They are herbivores feeding on seeds, fruits, flowers and nectar primarily. They also feed on insects.

SORA
Breeding

Breeding occurs from May to July. The female then lays 10 to 12 eggs that are incubated for around 19 days. Both parents take turns to incubate the eggs. Upon hatching, the young are fully developed and are able to walk and swim within the first day. Both parents take part in caring for the young. Once they are 4 weeks old, they become independent.

Appearance

Sora birds have dark-marked brown upper parts and a blue-green face and under parts. They have black and white bars on their faces. They also have short bills that are yellow in color and black markings are present on their faces. Their faces are white in color while their breast area is buff. Adults weigh about 49 to 112 grams.

Length

Adults range in length fromn19 to 30 centimeters and have a wingspan of 35 to 40 centimeters.

Diet

They feed on snails, spiders, crustaceans, beetles, flies, grasshoppers and dragon flies. They also feed on sedges, bulrushes, smartweeds and barnyard grasses.

WHISKERED TERN
Breeding

Whiskered terns attain sexual maturity when they are around 2 years old. Breeding occurs from May to June. The female then lays 2 to 3 eggs which are incubated for 18 to 20 days. Both parents care for the young until they fledge and become independent.

Appearance

Whiskered terns are slender and medium-sized terns that have a mid-grey appearance on their upper parts, tail and rump. Their under parts are grey while their belly has a dark coloration. Their tails are short and exhibit slight forking. They also have dark brown irises, a dark red bill and red legs. Adults weigh 60 to 100 grams with males being larger than females.

Lifespan

They live for a maximum of 16 years in the wild.

Length

Adults measure about 26 centimeters in length and have a wingspan of 65 to 70 centimeters.

Diet

They are carnivores feeding on small fish, insects, insect larvae, crustaceans and amphibians.

MUTE SWAN
Breeding

Mute swans attain reproductive maturity when they are around 3 years old. Breeding occurs from March to April. The female then lays 5 to 12 pale grey to pale blue-green eggs which are incubated for 36 to 38 days. Both parents take turns to incubate the eggs with the female being the primary incubator while the male defends the nest. Upon hatching, both parents care for the young who fledge when they are 60 days old. The chicks remain with their parents until they are a year old at which time they become independent.

Appearance

Both male and female mute swans have a similar appearance with both having a white plumage. Their bills are orange in color and have a knob at the base. The tips of these bills as well as the base are black. Adults weigh 7600 to 14300 grams with males being larger than females.

Lifespan

They can live for about 10 years in the wild.

Length

Adults range from 144 to 158 centimeters in length and have a wingspan of 2 to 2.5 meters.

Diet

They are primarily herbivores feeding on leaves, algae, roots and tubers. They also feed on mollusks, insects and aquatic worms.

GAMBEL'S QUAIL
Breeding

Gambel's quails become reproductively mature when they are around one year old. Breeding occurs from April. The female then lays around 10 to 12 white eggs that have brown spots. These are incubated for 22 to 23 days solely by the female although if the female dies, the male incubates the eggs. Upon hatching, both parents take part in caring for the young. Until they fledge and become independent.

Appearance

Females are dull in appearance having thin plumes while males have thick dark plumes. They also have a black face and neck and their breast has a black patch. Their sides are chestnut colored and their wings are olive with various white and cream markings. Adults weigh 160 to 200 grams.

Lifespan

In the wild, they live for about 7 years.

Length

Adults measure about 28 centimeters in length and have a wingspan of 36 to 41 centimeters.

Diet

They are herbivores feeding on shrubs, grasses, berries, cactus fruit and seeds.

WILSON'S SNIPE
Breeding

Breeding occurs from April to August. The female then lays 2 to 4 eggs that are incubated for 18 to 20 days. Females are the primary incubators although males also take part in incubating the eggs. Both parents care for the young for several weeks until they fledge and become independent.

Appearance

Wilson's snipe birds have buff and brown stripes and bars that are intricately patterned. Their heads are dark and have prominent whitish to buff stripes. They also have a dark back with three long streaks that are buff colored. These birds have a buff chest that has streaks and is spotted with brown. The sides of their bodies are heavily black barred. When in flight, their wings appear dark both above and below. Adults weigh 79 to 146 grams.

Lifespan

In the wild, they live for around 6 years.

Length

Adults range in length between 23 to 28 centimeters and have a wingspan of 39 to 45 centimeters.

Diet

They are primarily carnivores feeding mostly on insects such as beetles and horse flies, earthworms, spiders, frogs, crustaceans and leeches. Some omnivorous variants also feed on leaves, berries and seeds.

HAWAIIAN CROW
Breeding

Hawaiian crow females become reproductively mature when they are 2 to 3 years of age while males attain sexual maturity at around 4 years. Breeding occurs from March to July. The female then lays 1 to 5 greenish-blue eggs which she solely incubates for 19 to 22 days. Upon hatching, both parents care for the young who fledge when they are 40 days old. They however remain dependent on their parents until they are around 8 months old at which time they become independent.

Appearance

The plumage of Hawaiian crow is brownish black and long, they possess bristly throat feathers and have black bills, feet and legs. Their wings appear lighter as compared to the rest of their bodies. Their bills are thick and their wings are rounded in shape. Females appear smaller and lighter than males. Adults weigh about 520 grams.

Lifespan

They live for 18 to 28 years.

Length

Adults range in length from 48 to 50 centimeters.

Diet

They are omnivores feeding on land snails, arachnids, isopods, flowers, fruits, small birds and nectar.

GREEN HERON
Breeding

Green herons attain reproductive maturity when they are around one year old. Breeding occurs from March to July. The female then lays 2 to 4 eggs which are incubated for 19 to 21 days. Both parents take part in caring for the young once they hatch. At around 16 to 17 days of age, the young fledge. They then remain with their parents until they are 30 to 35 days old at which time they become independent.

Appearance

Green herons have small and stocky bodies with adults having a glossy green-black cap and back. They have black wings that are blue to green on the edges. They also have grey under parts. These birds have dark bills and orange legs. Juvenile birds have a neck and chest appearance that is comprised of white and brown stripes. Their backs are brown with white and beige spots. Adults weigh about 175 grams with males being larger than females.

Lifespan

They live for up to 8 years in the wild.

Length

Adults range in length from 41 to 46 centimeters and have a wingspan of 64 to 68 centimeters.

Diet

They are carnivores feeding on grasshoppers, water bugs, crayfish, sunfish, catfish, perch, goldfish, eels, rodents, lizards, tadpoles, frogs and snakes.

HORNED PUFFIN
Breeding

Horned puffins attain reproductive maturity when they are 5 to 7 years old. Breeding occurs from May to September. The female then lays one egg which is oval in shape and has an off-white appearance with grey, brown and lavender markings. The egg is incubated by both patents for up to 41 days. Upon hatching, the chicks receive care from both parents. They fledge once they are 40 days old and become independent thereafter.

Appearance

They are medium-sized birds whose plumage varies in the breeding and non-breeding season. Outside the breeding season, they have a grey-black appearance above which becomes brownish-grey below. Their bills are small in size and their faces adopt a smoky greyish brown appearance in front that becomes silver grey in the back. During the breeding season, these birds are black in color and a large white patch is present on either side of their faces. They also have white under parts that are found from the breast area to their tail feathers. Their bills are large in size and bright yellow to redo range with a red tip. Their legs range from yellow-orange to red and their eyelids are red too. Immature birds resemble the adult plumage outside the breeding season but their faces are smoky black and their bills are greyish-brown and short. Adults weigh 400 to 600 grams.

Lifespan

They live for over 20 years.

Length

Adults measure 36 to 41 centimeters in length and have a height of around 20 centimeters. They have a wingspan of around 58 centimeters.

Diet

They are carnivores feeding primarily on fish. They also feed on squid, crustaceans, small invertebrates and polychaete worms. They also consume algae and marine plants.

PLANTS

NONI
Description

Noni is a small-sized evergreen tree or shrub with pinnate veined leaves that have a glossy surface. The leaves are arranged opposite to each other and grow up to 12 inches long. They have an elliptical shape with a membranous blade. These plants produce white flowers that have ovoid heads. They grow to a height of 3 to 10 meters.

Fruit

They produce yellowish-white fruits that are fleshy measuring up to 10 centimeters long and around 3 to 4 centimeters in diameter. The fruit is initially green, it then turns yellow and becomes white upon ripening.

Uses

The plant is used to make juice drinks, cosmetic products such as lotions, the powder from their leaves is used for encapsulation. Its leaves are used as food and its fruit, although bitter, was consumed during famine. The fruit is also added to salad. The plant was also used in traditional medicine and its fruit was used to manufacture dye.

THATCH SCREWPINE
Description

Thatch screw pine is a small-sized tree that usually has a brown ringed single trunk. The trunk measures about 12 to 25 centimeters wide. The bark of these plants ranges in color from greyish to reddish brown and has a smooth to flaky appearance. It produces dark green leaves that measure up to 90 to 150 centimeters long and may have spines along the edges and the ribs throughout the leaves. The leaves of these plants usually have a spiral arrangement. Female flowers have a pineapple-like appearance and are surrounded by big white bracts while male flowers are white, tiny and in clusters with a fragrance. It grows to a height of 4 to 14 meters.

Fruit

The fruit resembles a pineapple and has an ovoid shape. It ranges in diameter from 4 to 20 centimeters.

Uses

Its fruit and seeds are edible and its leaves were used to make mats, baskets, outrigger canoe sails and thatch roofs. The male flowers are used in the manufacture of perfumes due to their fragrance.

STRAWBERRY GUAVA
Description

Strawberry guava is a small sized tree that has a smooth bark which ranges in color from grey to reddish-brown. This plant bears elliptical leaves that are dark green, aromatic and measure up to 4.5 centimeters in length. Its flowers grow either singly or in clusters of around 3 and are produced from October to December. Strawberry guava grows up to 20 feet in height.

Fruit

It produces strawberry guavas which are bright red fruits that are round to oval in shape and range from 2 to 4 centimeters in diameter.

Uses

Its fruit is edible and can be eaten or used in the manufacture of juices and jam. Its leaves may also be used to make tea. The wood of strawberry guava is used for lathe work, to make charcoal and firewood and in making tool handles. The beads of individual fruits are used to make necklaces.

AUTOGRAPH TREE
Description

Autograph tree is an evergreen tree that is wide spreading with a rounded crown. Its trunk is short while its crown is densely foliated. The leaves of autograph tree are thick with a dull green

appearance on the upper surface and an olive green appearance on the underside. They measure about 7 to 15 centimeters long. Flowering occurs all year round with a peak in summer. The flowers are white in color and open at night and on cloudy days but may remain open all morning. The flowers are about 5 to 7 centimeters across. It grows to a height of 7 to meters and 4 to 7 meters wide.

Fruit

They bear light green fruits that are poisonous and measure about 7 centimeters wide. When ripe, the fruits turn black and split to release bright red seeds.

Uses

Autograph tree has ornamental value when planted in gardens and has also been used for medicinal purposes. Its leaves were used to make playing cards and in making game balls. It is also a source of tar and firewood.

CANDLENUT
Description

Candlenut produces pale green leaves that may be ovate to heart-shaped. These leaves measure about 20 centimeters long and 13 centimeters wide. Young leaves may have rusty to cream stellate hairs. It produces small flowers with female flowers being around 9 millimeters in length while male flowers are around 5 millimeters. It grows to a height of around 30 meters.

Fruit

Its fruit is a drupe which is about 4 to 6 centimeters wide with one to two lobes.

Uses

Its nut is cooked or toasted and is used in curries and in making a thick sauce which is eaten with rice and vegetables. The nut is

mildly toxic when it is raw. Its wood was used to make coffins of the wealthy among the Batak people. The fruit and tree were used as a property-line manager and its fruit was used in tattoo-making as an ingredient for the ink. It has been used in ancient Hawaii to make 'inamona' which was made from roasted candlenuts. The nuts were also burned in ancient Hawaii to produce light. Hawaiian fishermen would chew its nuts and spit them on to water to enhance underwater visibility. A coating of candlenut oil was also used to preserve their fishing nets.

AUSTRALIAN UMBRELLA TREE
Description

Australian umbrella tree is a multi-trunked evergreen tree that produces compound leaves that are about 40 centimeters long.

 Its trunk is grey and has a smooth surface. Its flowers are red in color and grow in an umbrella-like pattern above the leaves. These trees grow to a height of around 15 meters.

Fruit

It produces a dark red fruit that is about 3 to 5 millimeters long and has a single seed. The seeds are pale brown and oval.

Uses

It is commonly used as landscape tree in Hawaii. Its fruits are consumed by birds, bats and rats. It also acts as a windbreaker.

COOK PINE
Description

It is a conical tree that has a slender spine-like crown. Its bark peels off in thin paper-like strips and is rough, grey and resinous. Its branches are quite short and in whorls around its slender trunk. These have cord-like branchlets that are horizontal. The branchlets have small green incurved and pointed tips with overlapping leaves that are spirally arranged. Cook pine grows to a height of around 60 meters.

Fruit

It produces cones and the male cones are cylindrical and pollen bearing while female cones are broad, ovoid and woody with spiny scales. The cones mature from green to brown after which they disintegrate and disperse their seeds.

Uses

It is a source of timber and is used in making furniture and bowls. Its seeds are consumed. The plant also has ornamental value and is planted in gardens as well as in public landscapes.

BITTER MELON
Description

Bitter melon is an herbaceous tendril-bearing vine which grows to a length of 5 meters. It produces simple alternate leaves that are around 4 to 12 centimeters across and have up to seven deeply separated lobes. They flower from June to July producing yellow male and female flowers on separate plants.

Fruit

It produces a fruit with a warty exterior and an oblong shape. Fruits are produced from September to November. They are edible.

Uses

It is cooked when it is in the green or early yellowing stage. Its leaves and young shoots are consumed as greens. It has also been used in soups and herbal teas and is also used in herbal medicine.

SEA ALMOND
Description

Sea almond is an upright tree that usually has a symmetrical crown. It produces large leaves that are broad, ovoid and glossy-dark-green and leathery leaves. These leaves are deciduous in the dry season and prior to falling, they turn yellow-brown. It bears both male and female flowers on the same plant and these range from white to greenish in color and are inconspicuous. It grows to a height of up to 35 meters.

Fruit

Its fruit is a drupe that is long and broad measuring about 5 to 7 centimeters long and 3 to 5 centimeters wide. It is usually green initially turning yellow and finally becomes red upon ripening. It usually has a single seed.

Uses

It has ornamental value and produces an edible fruit. Its seeds are also edible both wen raw and when cooked. Its wood is used in making canoes and its leaves were used in traditional medicine in the treatment of liver disease, and its herbal tea in treating diarrhea and dysentery. The leaves are believed to contain agents for cancer prevention.

BRAZILIAN PEPPER
Description

Brazilian paper is an evergreen shrub that bears dark-green leaves. The leaves have prominent pale veins above and have a pale and smoother appearance beneath. The leaflets appear rounder. These plants bear small sized creamy flowers from September to March with male and female flowers developing on separate trees. They grow to a height of around 6 meters.

Fruit

They produce bright red spherical drupes carried in clusters of up to 100 berries that are fleshy and contain a single seed.

Uses

They have an ornamental value, and in the treatment of gout, menstrual disorders, gonorrhea, gingivitis, sores, swellings, urethritis, ulcers, warts and wounds in herbal medicine. A liquid extract prepared from the bark is used as a stimulant and a tonic.

ZULU GIANT
Description

Zulu giant usually has green stems that are about 3 centimeters thick and its blooms are usually large and star-shaped with flowers that have five petals and measure about 25 centimeters in diameter. Its flowers can be yellow or red and are wrinkled with a silky texture. The flowers appear in autumn. These plants usually have a bad smell and grow to a height of around 20 centimeters.

RAINBOW GUM
Description

Rainbow gum is a fast-growing tree with a smooth, orange-tinted bark which sheds in strips to reveal streaks that are pale

green, red, orange, purplish brown and grey. Their branchlets have square cross-sections. It produces flower buds in a branching inflorescence in leaf axils with mature buds being pale green to cream with a roughly spherical shape. These trees grow to a height of 60 to 75 meters.

Fruit

It produces a woody, brown hemispherical capsule that is around 3 to 5 millimeters in length with three to four valves extending beyond the rim of the fruit. The fruits contain up to 12 minute brown seeds.

Uses

It is used to make pulpwood for making white paper and also has ornamental value.

MAMAKI
Description

Mamaki is a shrub that is native to Hawaiian Islands. It produces light green leaves that have a white appearance on the underside. Their leaves are around four inches to one foot and have a rough texture. Their flowers are inconspicuous. It grows to a height of 5 to 15 feet tall.

Fruit

It produces fleshy white fruits with each fruit containing numerous tiny brown seeds.

Uses

Hawaiians used the plant for its healing benefits and the plant is considered sacred due to its ability to cure various delibilities. It is used to treat ulcers and digestive disorders and in blood building, lowering cholesterol, relieving digestive disorders and in supporting a woman's body during childbirth.

GLORY BUSH
Description

It is an evergreen shrub with broad oval shaped leaves that are velvety and measures around 4 to 12 centimeters long and 2 to 5 centimeters wide. Its leaves are usually dark-green on the upper surface and have a lighter appearance beneath. It produces purple flowers that are 20 to 40 millimeters long. It grows to a height of 1 to 4 meters. Flowering occurs in fall, spring and summer. Glory bush grows to a height of around 6 to 8 feet and a width of around 3 to 5 feet.

Fruit

It produces inconspicuous brown fruits. The fruit is a small 5-parted round capsule which becomes brown upon attaining maturity.

Uses

Infusions of the plant have been used for stomach problems. It is also planted in gardens for its ornamental value.

TRUMPET TREE
Description

It is a softwood tree that grows to a height of 30 feet and bears dull green leaves that grow in an alternate fashion and are usually large and thick with an umbrella-like appearance. The leaves are about 30 to 76 centimeters long and are clustered at tips of the stems that are inward-curving. Its trunk has a grey smooth surfaced bark which is often ringed with leaf scars. It produces a sparsely branched canopy and sometimes develops prop roots around its base.

Fruit

Its fruits are in form of elongated pods that release winged seeds upon splitting.

Uses

It produces light to medium weight wood that is a source of timber. Its roots provide wood which is used for floats, inner soles of shoes and razor strops. It also has ornamental value and is grown as a honey plant by bee keepers.

PROSTRATE SANDMAT
Description

It is an annual herb that bears oval-shaped leaves that are about a centimeter long and have finely toothed edges. It also has hairy leaves and stems and its stem can be up to 7 to 8 inches long. The stem spreads to form a mat of up to 16 inches in diameter. It produces white to pinkish flowers that are regular in round clusters from June to September. The flowers are cup-shaped and have white petal-like structures around them. It grows to a height of 2 to 3 inches.

Fruit

Its fruit is a tiny 3-lobed hairy egg-shaped capsule that is pale brown.

Uses

It is effective in the treatment of bleeding hemorrhoids and has also been used in the treatment of breathing disorders such as asthma and bronchitis.

WILD LEADWORT
Description

Wild leadwort is an evergreen shrub that is multi-stemmed. It bears branches that are sender and these can be climbing, erect or prostrate. Its leaves have a pale-green appearance above that becomes greyish underneath. The leaves are arranged in an alternating pattern on the stems and have ovate to lance-elliptic blades. The flowers of these plants have white corollas and are produced all-year round. Wild leadwort can grow to a height of 1 meter.

Fruit

Its fruit is a capsule.

Uses

It has medicinal uses with its powdered roots being used in the treatment of piles and diarrhea. It also helps in boosting immunity and reducing inflammation. Traditionally, it was used in the treatment of warts and wounds. Its flowers are edible and it also has ornamental value.

BLACK WATTLE
Description

Black wattle is a round evergreen tree that has branches that are shallow ridged. It usually has fine hairs and a smooth bark that is grey and becomes black and fissured. It then splits to release gum. Its leaves are dark dull olive-green and densely packed together. It also bears cream-colored flowers.

Fruit

Its fruit is black to reddish brown pods that measure 4 to 8 millimeters.

Uses

Its gum was used as food and in the making of cement. Its bark was also used to make coarse strings and ropes. It is also infused in water and used as medicine for indigestion.

ACORN PEPEROMIA
Description

It is a low-growing shrub that has creeping stems. It produces elliptical to round leaves that grow in whorls of 3 to 4 and are typically green but may also be reddish on their underside. It grows to a height of 10 to 30 centimeters and spreads about 60 centimeters.

OLOMEA
Description

Olomea is a small tree that produces shiny ovate leaves which have red veins. These are attached in an alternating fashion on the branches. The branches of these trees have a red appearance. The plant produces greenish flowers that mature into fruits. It grows to a height of 2 to 8 meters tall.

Fruit

The fruit of olomea is red colored berries.

Uses

Its wood is used as a fire stick and is rubbed in a groove of a softer wood so as to ignite the particles of the softwood.

PORTIA TREE
Description

Portia tree is an evergreen shrub that produces heart-shaped leaves that are shiny dark-green above and measure about 5 to 20 centimeters. Its young branches have a brown scaly appearance. It produces hibiscus-like flowers with a yellow corolla and a red center that turns maroon by night. It grows to a height of around 40 feet and its trunk measures about 20 to

30 centimeters in diameter.

Fruit

Its fruit is a globose, flattened and 5-parted capsule that is about 4 centimeters wide and yellow in color but turns black after sometime.

Uses

It is used in woodworks commonly in the manufacture of bowls in Hawaii. In certain cultures, the tree was regarded as being sacred and was also used for religious sculpture. It is also used in making slotted wooden drums and hourglass drums.

COMMON LANTANA
Description

Common lantana is a small broad-leafed evergreen shrub with woody stems. Its leaves are broad, ovate and arranged in an alternating pattern. They usually produce a strong odor upon being crushed. Its flowers are tubular shaped and range in color from red, yellow, pink, orange and white.

Fruit

Its fruit is a berry-like drupe that turns from green to dark purple upon attaining maturity. Unripe fruits are inedible.

Uses

Its stalks are used in furniture construction. It has medicinal value and is used in the treatment of skin itches, cancer, measles, chicken pox, asthma, measles, leprosy and ulcers. Common lantana is also grown for its ornamental value.

MADAGASCAR RAGWORT
Description

Madagascar ragwort is a smooth stemmed herb that grows in an erect fashion. Its leaves grow alternately and are narrow lanceolate to elliptical in shape. They have bright green smooth margins that can be entire, lobed or serrated. The leaves measure about 2 to 7 centimeters long and 3 to 10 millimeters wide. Madagascar ragwort produces small yellow daisy-like flowers that are about 1 to 2 centimeters in diameter. Blooming occurs from late autumn to early spring. Madagascar ragwort grows to a height of round 20 to 60 centimeters.

Fruit

Its fruit is an achene that is brown in color and measures 1.5 to 2.5 millimeters long.

Uses

These plants have no ornamental or medicinal value.

SUGI

Description

It is an evergreen tree that is large in size with a trunk diameter of about 4 meters. Its bark is red-brown and peels in vertical stripes. Its leaves are needle-like and pale green with a spiral arrangement measuring about 0.1 to 1 centimeter long. It grows to a height of 70 meters and usually has a conical crown.

Fruit

It produces brown to dark brown globular seed cones that are around 1 to 2 centimeters in diameter and contain 20 to 40 scales.

Uses

It is a source of construction materials, furniture, fences, wooden clogs, shipbuilding, and ceiling panels. It is used in the manufacture of sugi essential oil that is believed to have soothing and calming effects. The oil is also used as a skincare product.

BE-STILL TREE
Description

It is an evergreen shrub that grows in an upright manner. Its leaves are bright green and glossy with entire margins and measure about 6 inches in length. The leaves also possess distinct midribs. It produces yellow or orange-yellow trumpet-like flowers that are around 1 to 3 inches in size. The flowers are also fragrant. It blooms in fall and summer. It grows to a height of 20 to 30 feet and has a diameter of 4 to 5 feet.

Fruit

Its fruit is nut-like seeds that are green initially and turn black upon attaining maturity.

Uses

It is planted for its ornamental value and is planted in gardens and parks for this reason. It is also used for biological pest control.

171

PIGEON BERRY

Pigeon berry is an erect evergreen vine-like herb whose leaves are about 15 centimeters long and 9 centimeters wide with a light green blade and thin texture. They are oval in shape and entire with a wavy margin. Their base is round while the apex is acuminate. The lower surface of the leaves may have few tiny hairs along the midrib and the main veins. It produces flowers that are initially white to pinkish and turn green as they mature. The flowers are around 2 to 3 millimeters in diameter. Its stem is greenish in color and soft when young. The stem is usually hairless.

Fruit

It produces small, glossy bright red berries that are around 2.5 to 5 millimeters in diameter. These turn from green to bright red upon attaining maturity.

Uses

Pigeon berry is cultivated for its ornamental value and as a shade-tolerant ground cover. Juice extracted from berries was used in manufacturing dye and ink. Studies have shown that its leaves and stems may have antimicrobial, analgesic, anti-inflammatory, anti-diabetic, anticancer and hepato-protective effects.

SHIPMAN'S CYANEA
Description

Shipman's cyanea is classified as a rare species. It is an unbranched to few-branched shrub that bears stalked leaves that are deeply cut into up to 20 to 30 lobes per leaf. The leaves measure between 6 to 12 inches long and 2 to 5 inches wide. Its flowers grow in clusters of 10 to 15 flowers and are covered with fine hairs. The flowers usually have pale greenish-white petals that are 3 to 3.6 centimeters long and fused into a curved five-lobed tube. That is 3 to 4 millimeter wide. It grows to a height of 2.5 to 4 meters.

Fruit

It produces small orange ellipsoid berries that have numerous small seeds.

WOODLAND STRAWBERRY
Description

It produces evergreen leaves that are coarse toothed with prominent veins and have an oval to egg-shaped appearance with a rounded tip and a tapered base. These measure around 1 inch long and 0.75 inches wide. Flowering occurs from April to June at which time they produce clusters of 2 to 5 flowers that are around half an inch wide and have 5 oval to round white petals. Present where the flower stalks diverge at the top of the stem is a small leaflet-like bract. It usually spreads by means of runners.

Fruit

It produces small red strawberries that are egg-shaped to conic and these contain tiny seeds that are raised on their surface.

Uses

Its fresh leaves were used to brew tea. The leaves were also chewed and applied as a poultice to burns. Tea made from the plant was also used in the treatment of diarrhea, regulating menstruation, promoting breast milk production, calming morning sickness. Its leaves were used as prevention for cold and in the treatment of anemia.

HIGHBUSH BLACKBERRY
Description

High brush blackberry is a woody shrub that usually has thorns on its stems, flowers and leaves. Its canes ranges from light green to dark red and are stout, ridged with sharp pricks. Its leaflets range from elliptic to oval in shape and are sharply toothed. The upper surface of the leaflets is medium green to yellowish green and indented along the veins. It often ranges from being hairless to being sparsely haired. The lower leaf surface is hairless between the veins. A pair of linear stipules is present at the base of each petiole. The canes of these plants grow to a height of around 80 inches.

Fruit

It produces compound drupes that are bright red initially and become black once they attain maturity.

Uses

Its leaves were used in the treatment of digestive problems such as diarrhea. When dried, the leaves are used to make tea.

BEACH MORNING GLORY
Description

Beach morning glory is a creeping vine that trails along the ground and may reach a width of 30 feet. Its leaves are elliptical to oval and lobed with a leathery texture and its stem is smooth. It produces funnel shaped white flowers with yellow centers which open in the morning and close by afternoon. Flowers are produced from early summer to fall. It attains a height of around 4 to 6 inches.

Fruit

Its fruit is a capsule that contains four hairy seeds.

Uses

Beach morning glory was used as poultice for stone fish strings. It was used in traditional medicine to treat gastrointestinal disorders and inflammation and in treating colic, edema, rheumatism, whitlow and piles.

KIAWE
Description

It is a small to medium-sized tree that grows to a height of 9 to 18 meters and is around 0.5 meters wide. Its bark is grey-brown and finely fissured with the outer bark being brown while the inner bark is orange brown. Its twigs are green, hairless and slightly zigzag with nodes at the leaf bases. Leaves are arranged in an alternating fashion and are finely haired with a dull light green appearance. They measure about 3 inches long. It produces flowers in clusters and these are usually light yellow with a cup-like five-toothed calyx. Flowers are mostly produced in spring and summer.

Fruit

Its fruit is bean-like, yellowish and slightly flattened measuring 3 to 8 inches long. It usually contains 10 to 20 seeds that are bean-like, elliptical and slightly flattened with a shiny brown appearance.

Uses

In Hawaii, it is used to make cement floats and mallets and in making heavy rifle stocks in match shooting. It is also used in making charcoal, fence posts and fuel wood. He pods are used as food for livestock and its flowers are a source of nectar for bees.

STINKING PASSION FLOWER
Description

It is a climbing vine that usually has sticky hairs with leaves having 3 to 5 pointed lobes. Its flowers are passion fruit-like and have cream colored petals with white to pink or purple centers. The flowers measure about 5 to 6 centimeters in diameter.

Fruit

Its fruit is globose and measures 2 to 3 centimeters in diameter. When ripe, fruits from the white flowered type of stinking passion flower are yellow and those from the pink flowered type are red.

Uses

Its fruit is edible as is its plant tips and young leaves. Its dry leaves were used in traditional medicine as tea and to relieve sleep problems, itching and coughs.

Made in United States
Troutdale, OR
05/03/2024

19600626R00104